How did I get this problem?

Social Responsibility Therapy: Understanding Harmful Behavior Workbook 1

James M. Yokley, Ph.D.

This workbook focuses on developing an understanding of "The Risk Factor Chain" that led to unhealthy, harmful behavior. Case study examples and interventions used in each link of the Risk Factor Chain covered in this workbook are described in Chapter 2 of the Social Responsibility Therapy treatment manual and in The Clinician's Guide to Social Responsibility Therapy listed in the references section.

The Social Responsibility Therapy focus on Understanding Harmful Behavior through "The Problem Development Triad" includes a three workbook series designed to help individuals with harmful behavior problems understand how they got that problem, what kept it going and how it spread to other areas.

Workbook 1- **"How did I get this problem?"** focuses on understanding how unhealthy, harmful behavior was acquired through The Risk Factor Chain

Workbook 2- **"Why do I keep doing this?"** focuses on understanding how unhealthy, harmful behavior problems were maintained by The Stress-Relapse Cycle

Workbook 3- **"How did my problem spread?"** focuses on understanding how unhealthy, harmful behavior problems were generalized to other areas using The Harmful Behavior Anatomy

A Social Solutions Healthy Behavior Lifestyle Development Project

Social Responsibility Therapy Mission Statement:
"Reclaiming Dignity through Honesty, Trust,
Loyalty, Concern and Responsibility"

Information on Social Responsibility Therapy is available at www.srtonline.org.
The Social Responsibility Therapy treatment manual for adolescents and young adults,
Social Responsibility Therapy workbooks and The Clinician's Guide are available at
www.socialsolutionspress.com

Published by
Social Solutions Press
Post Office Box 444
North Myrtle Beach, South Carolina 29597
Forth printing

i

Who can benefit from this workbook?

Individuals with unhealthy, harmful behavior- Those who are uncertain of how they developed their harmful behavior can benefit from the "Structured Discovery" approach of this workbook with assistance from their therapist. In addition, those who are aware of some contributing factors but do not have a full understanding of "How did I get this problem?" are also likely to benefit. See summary on back cover.

Mental Health Professional use in treatment plans and programs- The Awareness Training Goal for those who complete this workbook is to understand how they acquired their problem behavior. The objectives are to complete each of the five links in "The Risk Factor Chain" and give at least one specific example of a healthy behavior success skill that can be used to address each personal risk factor. Since the focus of this workbook is on the primary contributing factors that allowed the client to acquire their harmful behavior, it is ideal for those who are not aware of a behavior pattern, state that, "It just started" or "I only did it once" and do not believe they have a harmful behavior cycle. The increased workbook structure includes step-by-step self-discovery directions. This "Structured Discovery" approach addresses the self-awareness problems exhibited by many individuals with unhealthy, harmful behavior. This Structured Discovery workbook is helpful for those with strong autonomy needs who value their independence, like to work on their own, take charge of their lives and help themselves deal with their own situations. It is ideal in limited resource public service or institutional settings that require group treatment by clients who must contribute to their treatment plans and support each others goals.

Harmful behavior is unhealthy, excessive, compulsive or abusive and harmful to self or others. Social Responsibility Therapy (SRT) has a strong focus on developing honesty, trust, loyalty, concern and responsibility as competing responses to harmful behavior. These multicultural prosocial values are the healthy relationship success skills that employers, parents, partners and probation/parole officers are looking for in their workers, children, relationships and parolees. SRT is highly consistent with the family values of faith-based treatment organizations as well as the "Right Living" treatment approach of Therapeutic Communities and Twelve-Step Programs. The SRT healthy relationship and behavior success skills focus meets the rehabilitation goals of correctional institutions and social service group homes making it easy to integrate into those settings. This workbook is best suited for individuals over age 13 with good reading ability and basic arithmetic skills. Although developed for use with therapist input to help those in treatment become more active participants, it can also provide self-awareness and motivation for those considering therapy. The three SRT workbooks on understanding harmful behavior were originally intended to be used consecutively but can used individually for treatment focused on insight (workbook 1), relapse prevention (workbook2) and co-occurring problems (workbook 3).

Mental health professional information on how to use this workbook is outlined in Appendix A. Workbook support materials listed in the references section include: A step-by-step clinician guide for implementing each workbook section and users guide for the healthy behavior success skills described in the workbook; A workbook development manual documenting the research support for each workbook section and; Social Responsibility Therapy treatment manuals for adults, adolescents and preteens.

Social Responsibility Therapy (SRT) Acknowledgements

A special thanks to: Christine Laraway and Brigette Bulanda for their help in implementing SRT with adolescents in Forensic Foster Care; Jennifer LaCortiglia for her help in adapting SRT for preteens; Rose Chervenak for her help in providing SRT to adolescents referred for sexual behavior problems in the residential Therapeutic Community setting; Chris Hewitt for his help in presenting Social Responsibility Therapy (SRT) to residential substance abuse clients and; Angie Roth for her program coordination of SRT for obesity patients in hospital-based treatment. Their feedback on the use of this workbook with clients exhibiting multiple forms of harmful behavior provided highly valuable treatment information.

| Understanding How Harmful Behavior was Acquired: |
| Social Responsibility Therapy Awareness Training Workbook 1 |

Table of Contents (continued)   Page

Introduction to Social Responsibility Therapy and Understanding Harmful Behavior

"If you're not working on the solution, you're part of the problem" -- Eldridge Cleaver [1]

Social Responsibility Therapy Summary

Social Responsibility Therapy addresses multiple forms of unhealthy, excessive, compulsive or abusive behavior that is harmful to self and/or others (i.e., "harmful behavior"). Traditional treatments typically focus on helping yourself. Social Responsibility Therapy focuses on developing a healthy balance between helping yourself and others. In Social Responsibility Therapy, learning to care for yourself and others involves developing enough social maturity (i.e., honesty, trust, loyalty, concern and responsibility) and emotional maturity (i.e., self-awareness, self-efficacy/confidence and self-control) to avoid behavior that is unhealthy to you or harmful to others. Social Responsibility Therapy teaches multicultural prosocial values and behaviors that help prevent unhealthy, harmful behavior. In Social Responsibility Therapy, "If you're not working on the solution, you're part of the problem". If part of the problem is that unhealthy, harmful behavior got in the way of your education, work on the solution by reading this workbook with a dictionary and educate yourself by looking up the words you don't know.

What's in it for me? Less unhealthy, harmful behavior results in less consequences and a more healthy, positive life. More unhealthy, harmful behavior leads to more consequences and a less healthy, negative life. Unless you are keenly aware of your thoughts, feelings and motivations, you will make decision mistakes or slips that lead to "relapse" and falling back into unhealthy, harmful behavior. One type of decision that leads to relapse involves a problem with awareness referred to as a "foresight deficit decision" or foresight slip. Foresight is the ability to look ahead and think about what could happen in different situations. A foresight deficit decision often results in thoughtless decisions to enter high risk situations for slipping into harmful behavior. If you were ever asked, "What were you thinking?" you probably had a foresight slip into trouble. This is a very serious matter. Since your decisions control the path that your life will take, you need to locate the type of harmful behavior you want to change or that resulted in your referral for treatment in Appendix B (p. 90) and study the examples of decisions that led to relapse by individuals who lacked foresight and self-awareness. Don't worry if the connection between the decisions and the relapse that occurred is not clear to you right now. The primary purpose of this workbook is to help you develop enough self-awareness to make those connections and avoid falling back into harmful behavior or developing a new one after you have successfully stopped this one. Although you can use this workbook as a self-help tool to develop your own awareness and understanding of yourself, it is typically used in individual/family therapy or in group treatment programs and you are likely to benefit from therapeutic discussion of each section with others. The unhealthy, harmful behavior targeted by Social Responsibility Therapy covers a broad spectrum of behavior on the Harmful Behavior Continuum (Table 1) ranging in Social Responsibility impact from primarily hurting self (e.g., excessive eating or skipping medication) to hurting self and others (e.g., substance abuse or gambling debt) to primarily hurting others (e.g., acts of physical or sexual aggression) and in severity from relatively mild to socially devastating. The multiple forms of abusive behavior that Social Responsibility Therapy targets includes sexual abuse (e.g., rape, child molestation, harassment), physical abuse (e.g., school bullying, assault, kidnapping, robbery), property abuse (e.g., theft, vandalism, arson, excess spending/shopping, gambling debt), substance abuse (e.g., drugs/alcohol, cigarettes, food) and trust abuse (e.g., lying, cheating, running away).

Table 1.
The Harmful Behavior Continuum: Selected Behavior Examples

Primary Area of Impact →

Behavior Impact Severity ↓

Harmful to Self	Harmful to Self and Others	Harmful to Others
Self Injury/Cutting		
Medication Non-compliance		
Food Abusers (Overeat/binge/purge/starve)		
Nicotine Abusers		
Workaholics (Single)	**Workaholics** (with partners or family)	
Codependents (Self-destructive relationships)	**Codependents** (Abuse enablers)	
Sexual Compulsives (Deviant masturbation, porno)	**Sexual Compulsives** (Unprotected sex, affairs, prostitution)	
Money Abusers (Single shopaholics)	**Money Abusers** (Gamblers with partners/family)	**Money Abusers** (Embezzlers, Credit fraud)
Substance Abusers (Single alcohol and drug abusers)	**Substance Abusers** (Alcohol and drug abusers with partners/family)	**Substance Abusers** (Drunk drivers, Drug dealers)
	Responsibility Abusers (Work Neglecters)	**Responsibility Abusers** (Child Neglecters)
	Trust Abusers (Partner cheating)	**Trust Abusers** (Professional con artist)
		Verbal/Power Abusers (employee harassment)
		Property Abusers (theft, vandalism, arson)
		Physical Abusers (bullying, assault, child abuse)
		Sexual Abusers (rape, child molestation)
		Contract Killers
		Lust Murderers, Serial Killers

Source: Adapted with permission from Table 1.1 in Yokley (2008)

Note: "The more difficult the problem, the harder it is to change" may not always be the case. Less severe harmful behaviors which impact less people can be more difficult to chance because of...

1. Impact Rationalization- It's low on the social impact continuum, e.g., "It doesn't hurt others, it only hurts me"
2. Availability and associated Normalization- It's normal to eat, smoke, spend and sometimes over do it, e.g., "Everyone does it" or "Lots of people do it". For example, smoking lapses "were more likely to occur when smoking was permitted, when cigarettes were easily available and in the presence of other smokers" (p. 64, Shiffman et. al., 1996).
3. Severity Minimization- It's the least on the severity continuum (above) and "It's not illegal". You can get arrested for drinking or drugging and driving but you can't get arrested for overeating and driving. We have a highway patrol and drug court but there is no buffet patrol and the only food court that exists is in the Mall.

In Social Responsibility Therapy, harmful behavior relates to a lack of social responsibility which is the result of a pathological level of social-emotional immaturity. Thus, a very basic summary of Social Responsibility Therapy is an intervention which develops honesty, trust, loyalty, concern and responsibility as competing factors against sexual abuse, physical abuse, property abuse, substance abuse and trust abuse. The main focus of Social Responsibility Therapy is on whether the action being considered is helpful or harmful to self or others. If it is helpful to self and others it is socially responsible and needs to be reinforced. If it is harmful to self and others it is socially irresponsible and needs to be re-directed. Three important treatment goals in Social Responsibility Therapy are to:

1. **Stop the harmful behavior**- Develop the healthy behavior success skills (p. 12) needed to keep from repeating unhealthy, harmful behavior;
2. **Understand the harmful behavior**- Develop awareness of how the unhealthy, harmful behavior was acquired, maintained and generalized to other problem areas and;
3. **Demonstrate helpful behavior**- Develop the healthy relationship success skills (p. 11) needed for positive social adjustment.

The focus of this workbook is on understanding unhealthy, harmful behavior and it is structured to help you discover how that behavior was acquired. The healthy behavior success skills you need to keep from repeating the problem (i.e., **A**void trouble; **C**alm down; **T**hink it through and; **S**olve the problem) are integrated into each workbook section. Developing healthy relationship success skills through honesty, trust, loyalty, concern and responsibility is also included.

Introspection 101: Becoming a Careful Self-Observer

Introspection means looking inside of yourself at your motivations for what you do which is the key to developing self-awareness. Becoming a careful observer of others and pointing out their problems is easy but you have to train yourself to look at your problem thoughts, feelings and motivations. Social Responsibility Therapy uses a Structured Discovery approach to help you look at yourself through *structured* exercises that help you *discover* important thoughts and feelings that are connected to unhealthy, harmful behavior. This process increases your self-awareness which develops your self-efficacy (confidence) and helps you maintain your self-control responsibility. Self-control is needed to achieve your personal goals and maintain successful relationships. The social responsibility of self-control tends to get overlooked in our school systems which teach effective control of baseballs, basketballs and footballs but leave it up to you to develop effective control of thoughts, feelings and behaviors.

Developing self-awareness through the structured discovery exercises in this workbook is like playing cards. Each section represents a hand of cards with different statements that may apply to you. Your job is to get honest with yourself by carefully looking at each statement for connections between that information and your behavior (like drawing a new card to see if it can be used in your hand). If the statement applies to you or adds to your understanding of yourself, mark it, if not let it go (discard) and move on to the next piece of information to consider (draw another card). Having the courage to accept the workbook statements that apply to you will allow you to put together a winning hand of connections between thoughts, feelings and motivations.

These connections will provide you with an understanding of how you got involved with your unhealthy, harmful behavior. If you are a mental health professional and are reviewing this workbook for use with your clients, information is provided for you in Appendix A (page 87).

There are two basic things that you can't change in life, the past and other people's behavior. As mentioned earlier, it has been said that "If you're not working on the solution, you're part of the problem". This is the case with many individuals with unhealthy, harmful behavior whose energy is too focused on the past and other people's behavior. Individuals who have problems with unhealthy, harmful behavior tend to spend far too much time ruminating (i.e., going over and over) on past injustices done to them by others, trying to cover up past mistakes of their own and trying to influence other people's opinions of them. This negative coping style maintains unhealthy pride, diverts energy away from solving your harmful behavior problem and makes you feel helpless since you can't change the past or other people's behavior.

In Social Responsibility Therapy, the focus is on the present and your behavior. While it is true that you can't change the past, you can change your honesty about it and understanding of it. Working on your honesty, trust, loyalty, concern and responsibility (which includes self-control) develops healthy pride and dignity. Understanding how you got this problem and learning the healthy behavior success skills to manage it are the first steps toward positive change. In order to successfully complete this workbook, you need to be willing to "set your pride aside" and use this workbook as a mirror to see yourself by carefully considering each statement. This begins with getting honest about past behavior that has been unhealthy to you or harmful to others.

History of Unhealthy, Harmful Behavior
"The more extensive a man's knowledge of what has been done,
the greater will be his power of knowing what to do" -- Benjamin Disraeli (1804-1881)

Review of Unhealthy, Harmful Behavior
Why go back through the past? That was then, this is now. What's in it for me to go through this again, other than bringing up bad memories? The answer is simple, to learn enough about the past to prevent your past history from repeating itself. In order to prevent history from repeating itself, you have to study history to make yourself aware of the problems and traps to avoid.

Circle all of the forms of harmful behavior on the Harmful Behavior Continuum (Table 1, p. 2) that you have ever been involved with in your life. Then complete the basic information about yourself below and then begin yourself understanding work.

Name: _____   **Date:** _____

Date of Birth: _____   Sex: _____   Race: _____

Education: _____   Occupation: _____   Marital Status: _____

Referral problem (What harmful behavior resulted in your referral for treatment or caused you to

get this workbook?): _____

Name of your current treatment program or provider: _____

Your current treatment Setting: __ Outpatient; __ Intensive Outpatient; __ Residential/Inpatient;

__ Secure Residential/Correctional Facility; __ Self-help, not in treatment

<u>Check all of the types of harmful behavior you have done</u>. Then underline the parts that apply to you.

____ Trust abuse- For example, lying, cheating, conning, coercion, fraud, running away, child neglect, walking out on a friend in need, shifting loyalties to others when it benefits you or when things aren't going well for current friends, using people for what they have, saying "I love (or really care about) you" just to get sex or justify having it. Making false allegations or filing false charges. Problem priorities- for example: Parents putting involvement in relationships before family/child care (see Planning Problems, p. 102); Putting negative associates before positive friends/family; Doing too much work and forgetting about relationships or getting too involved in relationships and forgetting about responsibilities; Putting other life tasks or relationships before treatment. Doing too much for others and not caring for yourself or getting too caught up in your problems and forgetting about others.

____ Responsibility neglect- Letting your responsibilities go and just doing what you want, what is easiest, what you feel like doing or what makes you feel good at the time. Putting off responsibilities until someone else does them, making excuses to avoid doing things you just don't want to do, Youth example- making excuses to miss or skip school/work, not completing activities that are required of you. Adult example- failure to pay bills or being an absent parent to your children (see Planning Problems, p. 102).

____ Responsibility abuse- Refusal to accept responsibilities. Examples include quitting school or job training, quitting a job without getting another job first, defaulting on loans, not paying people back, not paying child support, using "survival" as an excuse for drug dealing addiction to "easy money", using not being able to find a job that pays enough as an excuse to live off of others without working at all. Cover-up for others abuse, not saying anything.

____ Responsibility overdose- Over-involvement in work/workaholic and neglecting relationships or family. Falling into becoming responsible for everyone and everything all the time, resulting in others always calling on you to get things done or help them out and not taking time to care for yourself (see Need Problems, p. 102).

____ Food abuse (i.e., overeating/overweight, excessive eating/binging, purging or starving self)

____ Substance abuse- legal substances (e.g., alcohol, prescription medications, cigarettes/tobacco or other legal substances- List here _____).

____ Substance abuse- illegal substances (e.g., marijuana, cocaine, methamphetamine, heroin or other recreational/street drugs- List here _____).

____ Property abuse- legal activity including money abuse (e.g., credit card debt, excessive borrowing, gambling debt, compulsive gambling, overspending or shopaholic)

____ Property abuse- illegal activity (e.g., theft, vandalism, arson, forgery, black mail or extortion/getting money by threats, or other property abuse- List here _____).

____ Physical abuse- harm to self (e.g., cutting self, pulling hair out, excessive scratching, picking skin off, injury from banging head or punching walls, suicide attempt)

____ Physical abuse- harm to others (e.g., assault, domestic violence, robbery, kidnapping, school bullying, physical intimidation, child physical abuse/excessive physical punishment)

____ Sexual abuse- harm to self or others (e.g., rape, child sexual abuse/molestation, sexual harassment, exhibitionism/flashing, voyeurism/peeping, prostitution, pandering/pimping, excessive/compulsive sexual behavior including cruising for sex, promiscuity, affairs, pornography, deviant masturbation, dangerous sex, unprotected sex with people I just met)

____ Other problem behavior (list-_____)

Referral Behavior History- Use the space below to write a history of the harmful behaviors and events that resulted in your referral for treatment, got you thinking you need to change or resulted in someone close to you telling you that you need to change. Include: **who** (your behavior hurt, self, others, both, be specific, give names); **what** (your referral behavior was, the primary reason you were referred for or need treatment); **when** (you started it and how long it has gone on); **where** (you usually did it or where it occurs often) and; **why** (you think you did it, include anything you can think of that can start it).

Who: _____

_____

_____

What: _____

_____

_____

_____

When: _____

_____

_____

Where: _____

_____

_____

Why: _____

_____

_____

_____

Introduction to The Problem Development Triad
"The power of man has grown in every sphere, except over himself"
-- Sir Winston Churchill (1874- 1965)

Some individuals with harmful behavior have never had a reasonable period of abstinence or time in their life where they were free of harmful behavior. They were unable to successfully control their behavior because they never understood:

1. **How they got the problem** to begin with;
2. **Why they kept it up** and;
3. **How it spread** into other problem areas.

The Problem Development Triad components covered in this three workbook series will be used to help you understand the:

1. **Risk Factor Chain** that led to acquiring your harmful behavior- How you got the problem;
2. **Stress-Relapse Cycle** that maintained it- Why you kept it up once you started and;
3. **Harmful Behavior Anatomy** of factors that generalized it- How it spread to other problems.

When you have finished the material needed to complete the summary worksheet at the end of each workbook you will have a graphic representation of how you got your problem (workbook 1), kept it (workbook 2) and spread it to other problem areas (workbook3). A summary of "The Problem Development Triad" used in Social Responsibility Therapy is provided in Figure 1. In Social Responsibility Therapy, our number one responsibility as human beings is self-control. Learning to control unhealthy, harmful behavior is the first and most important step toward getting what you want in life. In the words of Dr. Albert Ellis "We are all fallible human beings" so having serious problems is not the issue. The issue is developing enough:

1. **social maturity** to hold yourself accountable about problems when mistakes are made and reclaim your dignity through honesty (see Healthy Relationship Success Skills, p. 11);
2. **emotional maturity** to learn from life mistakes by becoming aware of the high risk situations that trigger those mistakes (see Situational Risk Factors, p. 41) and;
3. **appropriate social behavior control** to stop unhealthy, harmful behavior using the Healthy Behavior Success Skills (see p. 12).

Crossroads- Life always has important crossroads and the path we choose determines the way our life will turn out. The crossroad in harmful behavior development is at the end of the Risk Factor Chain when you first started your harmful behavior. The Risk Factor Chain sets you up for harmful behavior and can lead to a number of types of interpersonal abuse (e.g., physical, verbal, sexual or trust abuse) or substance abuse (e.g., drugs, alcohol, cigarettes or food abuse). If an individual has enough risk factors in each link of the Risk Factor Chain to lead them into a harmful behavior, their use of positive or negative coping determines what happens next.

The Awareness Training goal at the end of this workbook is for you to understand how you got your problem behavior with enough confidence to be able to explain it clearly to others. In order to reach this level of understanding you will need to complete each of the five links in "The Risk Factor Chain" and be able to give at least one specific example of a healthy behavior success skill that you have used to address each personal risk factor. If you are able to understand

Figure 1. The Problem Development Triad:

(Managing these risk, stress and generalization problems is summarized in Exhibits 1-3, p. 84)

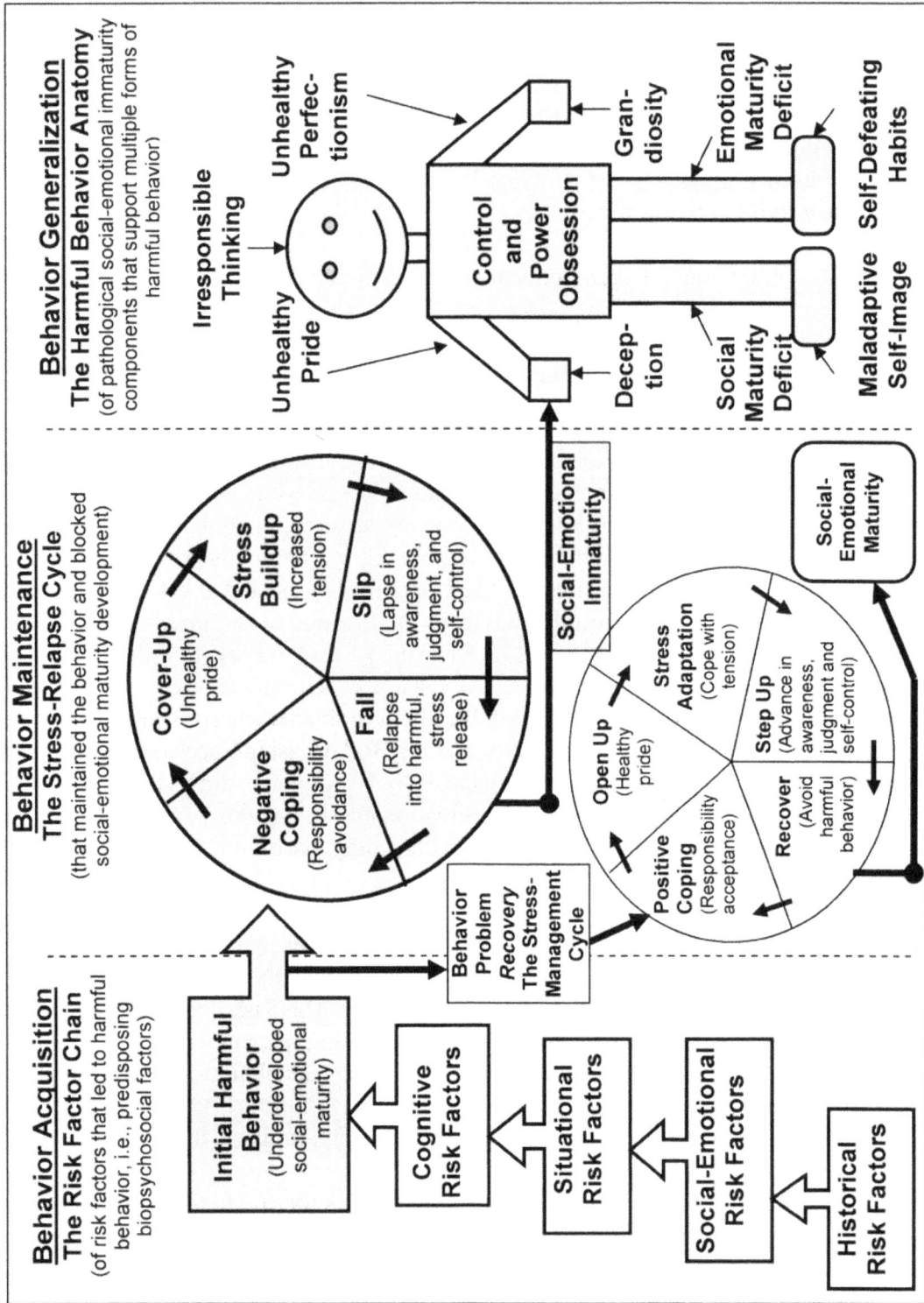

Figure 1. The Problem Development Triad: How Harmful Behavior Was Acquired, Maintained & Generalized Referred to as "The Abuse Development Triad" in cases of sexually and/or physically abusive behavior. Source: Yokley, 2008.

Behavior Generalization
The Harmful Behavior Anatomy
(of pathological social-emotional immaturity components that support multiple forms of harmful behavior)

Unhealthy Perfectionism
Irresponsible Thinking
Unhealthy Pride
Control and Power Obsession
Grandiosity
Emotional Maturity Deficit
Self-Defeating Habits
Deception
Social Maturity Deficit
Maladaptive Self-Image

Behavior Maintenance
The Stress-Relapse Cycle
(that maintained the behavior and blocked social-emotional maturity development)

Stress Buildup (Increased tension)
Slip (Lapse in awareness, judgment, and self-control)
Cover-Up (Unhealthy pride)
Fall (Relapse into harmful, stress release)
Negative Coping (Responsibility avoidance)

Social-Emotional Immaturity

Behavior Problem Recovery
The Stress-Management Cycle

Stress Adaptation (Cope with tension)
Step Up (Advance in awareness, judgment and self-control)
Open Up (Healthy pride)
Recover (Avoid harmful behavior)
Positive Coping (Responsibility acceptance)

Social-Emotional Maturity

Behavior Acquisition
The Risk Factor Chain
(of risk factors that led to harmful behavior, i.e., predisposing biopsychosocial factors)

Initial Harmful Behavior (Underdeveloped social-emotional maturity)
Cognitive Risk Factors
Situational Risk Factors
Social-Emotional Risk Factors
Historical Risk Factors

and address these factors, you will have successfully decreased your risk for developing a new behavior problem in addition to developing your confidence in managing your present problem.

Using positive coping is the more difficult path to take after a period of harmful behavior because admitting the problem can result in unwanted consequences. However, positive coping has the added advantages of:

- Developing **honesty** and letting go of unhealthy pride that makes it worse by covering up;
- Repairing broken **trust** and developing the positive relationships needed to stay on track;
- Reducing stress-build up from anxiety about getting caught or guilt about what you did by doing the right thing and being **loyal** to family values (what is right for yourself and others);
- Showing **concern** for yourself and others by keeping your problem up front and thinking ahead about the consequences of falling back into secret-keeping;
- Developing **responsibility** by holding yourself accountable and learning to solve problems by focusing on the present and your behavior, not the past and other people's behavior.

In summary, the drawbacks of positive coping are the consequences of honesty. Although "honesty has its price, the good news is that you don't have to pay twice". The advantages of positive coping include adapting to the stress of making mistakes by reclaiming your dignity through your honesty, trust, loyalty and responsibility. Positive coping leads to resilience (bouncing back) by learning from experience which develops social maturity and wisdom (see Figure 2). During the course of this workbook, you will develop your positive coping skills using the Situation Response Analysis Log in Appendix D (p. 107).

Figure 2. The Prevention or Development of Harmful Behavior

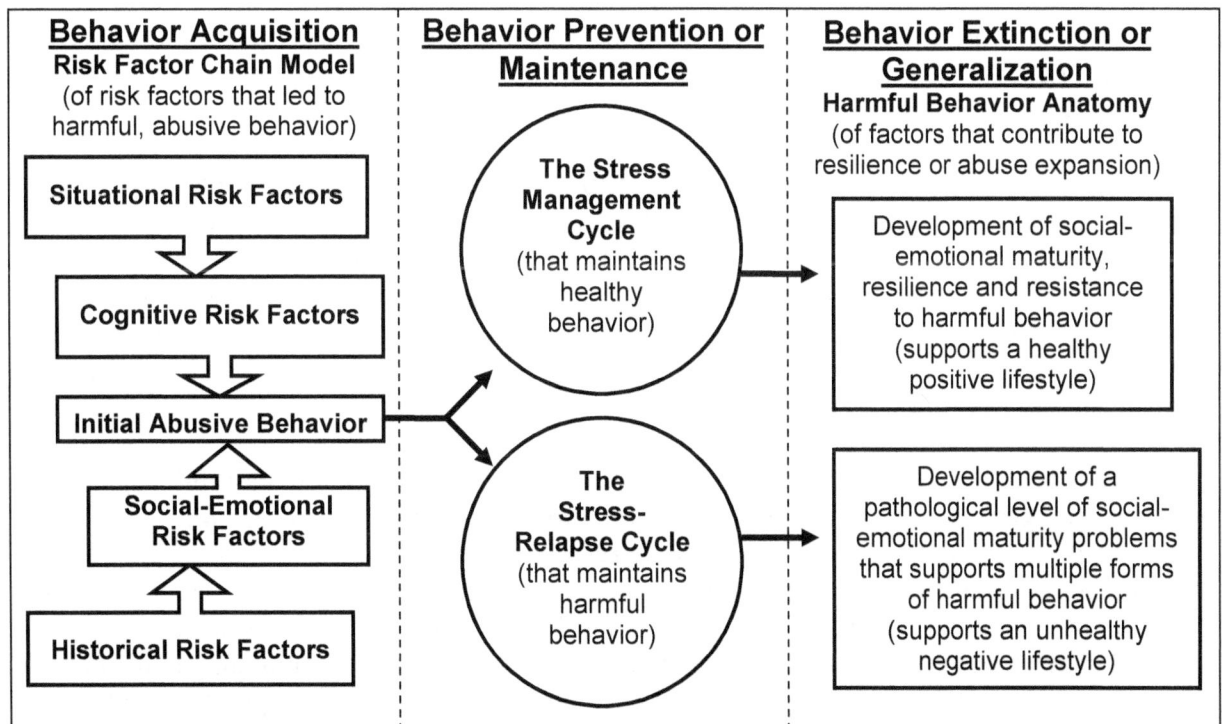

Behavior Acquisition	Behavior Prevention or	Behavior Extinction or
Risk Factor Chain Model (of risk factors that led to harmful, abusive behavior)	**Maintenance**	**Generalization** **Harmful Behavior Anatomy** (of factors that contribute to resilience or abuse expansion)

Situational Risk Factors

Cognitive Risk Factors

Initial Abusive Behavior

Social-Emotional Risk Factors

Historical Risk Factors

The Stress Management Cycle (that maintains healthy behavior)

The Stress-Relapse Cycle (that maintains harmful behavior)

Development of social-emotional maturity, resilience and resistance to harmful behavior (supports a healthy positive lifestyle)

Development of a pathological level of social-emotional maturity problems that supports multiple forms of harmful behavior (supports an unhealthy negative lifestyle)

Using negative coping, denying the problem, and covering it up by "acting as if" everything is alright, avoids dealing with the problem. Negative coping creates stress build-up. This eventually results in slipping up and taking a fall back into the Stress-Relapse Cycle that maintains unhealthy, harmful behavior (Figure 2, p. 9). Falling back into the cycle reinforces the social-emotional maturity problems that prevent learning from experience and supports multiple forms of harmful behavior that result in an unhealthy, unhappy, negative life. Over time, repeated relapse through the Stress-Relapse Cycle develops a level of social-emotional maturity problems that spreads one type of unhealthy, harmful behavior to other types or other areas of your life. Given this situation, the harmful behavior that brought you to treatment is often not your only harmful behavior. Also, the harmful behavior that resulted in your referral for treatment may not be the first harmful behavior that you developed. Examples include earlier alcohol abuse being in remission (now under control) but getting substituted with urges to take out feelings on others verbally and physically (i.e., the "dry drunk" syndrome). Earlier trust abuse (i.e., abusing the trust of others by lying, cheating, manipulating, conning, etc.) may go into remission (increasing boredom) but the excitement of trust abuse can get substituted by cocaine abuse. Perhaps excessive or risky sexual behavior is in remission but the untreated emotional maturity problem of self-control is now showing itself through excessive eating or risking money (gambling). Or maybe unhealthy overeating is in remission but is now being substituted with over-spending.

"Knowledge is power." The more we know about how we developed our present behavior patterns, what maintained that behavior and how it spread to other areas, the more confident we can be in understanding ourselves, understanding others, maintaining positive behavior change and achieving positive life goals. It takes a great deal of work to get a clear understanding of your unhealthy, harmful behavior. Not everyone will succeed. To achieve a positive lifestyle, developing self-understanding must include developing dignity through honesty, trust, loyalty, concern and responsibility. Not everyone will continue on the path to social responsibility. Those that do will develop the self-understanding that builds the self-confidence needed for self-control of unhealthy, harmful behavior and maintenance of a healthy, positive lifestyle.

Summary of Healthy Relationship and Behavior Success Skills

The awareness training focus of this workbook is on helping you understand how you acquired your harmful behavior through the Risk Factor Chain. During awareness training on how you got this problem, it is equally important to keep the problem under control. This requires a responsibility and tolerance training focus on: 1) the healthy behavior success skills needed to change that harmful behavior and; 2) the healthy relationship success skills needed to form a positive support network that will help maintain that positive change.

The healthy behavior success skills you need to keep from falling back into harmful, negative behavior are: **A**void trouble; **C**alm down; **T**hink it through and; **S**olve the problem.[2] The healthy relationship success skills you need for positive relationship development and to help you maintain behavior change are honesty, trust, loyalty, concern and responsibility. In relationships these are the things that we want from others in our life and that others want from us. Both healthy behavior and relationship success skills are needed for positive community adjustment and to get what you want in life. These skills are related to each other and support each other.

Healthy <u>Relationship</u> Success Skills (Description)

Honesty- Involves getting honest with yourself about your mistakes and with others about their mistakes. Tell yourself the truth about the feelings that others could have about your actions and how you feel about the actions of others. Getting honest involves learning to "Calm down" so that you don't justify lying based on fear of consequences (see p. 12- 13) and learning to "Think it through" by weighing out the severity of the consequences to yourself and others on the reality scales (see p. 13- 14). Confront deception (see p. 94) in yourself and others. List the benefits of honesty and how you can improve it. What could you do differently? Get others opinions.

_____

_____

Trust- Involves: 1) <u>building trust</u> in others by taking responsibility to "Avoid trouble" (see p. 12), keeping your word and respecting others feelings along with; 2) <u>learning to trust</u> others by opening up about problems and picking the right people to trust. Avoid trust double standards (see p. 94). List the benefits of trust, how you can improve it, what you can do. Gather opinions.

_____

_____

Loyalty- Involves <u>standing up for what you know is right</u> and who you know is right especially when there is social pressure to keep quiet, i.e., "If you don't stand for something, you'll fall for anything." This means learning to "Think it through" (see p. 13- 14) to avoid Irresponsible Loyalty by going along with what is wrong just to get along, compromising yourself to be accepted or covering up for others (see p. 96). List the benefits of loyalty and how you can improve your loyalty below. What could you do differently? Get others opinions.

_____

_____

Concern- Involves: 1) <u>helping self</u> by keeping problems "up front" as a daily priority so that they don't get out of control again; 2) <u>helping others</u> by treating them the way they want to be treated; 3) blocking helplessness by taking responsibility to "Solve the Problem" (see p. 14- 15) instead of blaming others (i.e., "when you blame other people for your behavior, you give them control over your life") and 4) substituting the "Don't care attitude" with the courage to care, share and try (see p. 96- 97). List the benefits of concern, how to improve, what you can do. Get opinions.

_____

_____

Responsibility- <u>Our number one responsibility is self-control</u> which involves learning to: **A**void trouble; **C**alm down; **T**hink it through and; **S**olve the problem (see p. 12- 16). Other important responsibilities are making things right (emotional restitution), pulling our own weight and learning to accept feedback. Getting what we want in life requires awareness of responsibility issues (see p. 97). List responsibility benefits, how to improve, what you can do. Get opinions.

_____

_____

Healthy <u>Behavior</u> Success Skills (Instructions)

Let's face it, most people who are completing a workbook on how they got their harmful behavior at one point in their lives have been told to avoid trouble or calm down or think things through before acting or that they need to solve their problem. This was telling you what you already know, not what you really need to know. What you really need to know is "how to" **A**void trouble, **C**alm down, **T**hink it through and **S**olve the problem.

How to **A**void trouble- If you have had some treatment experience in the past, you may have heard the skills used to avoid trouble referred to as "relapse prevention". These skills basically involve becoming aware of your high risk situations for relapse into unhealthy, harmful behavior and then making relapse prevention plans to avoid or escape those situations. The focus in this workbook will be on learning to apply one basic skill to avoid trouble, the 3-step social responsibility plan to: 1) get out of trouble, 2) get honest with yourself and 3) get responsible with your behavior. <u>Get out</u> (Remove yourself)- Involves getting out of the high risk situation by leaving without hesitation. No one thinks clearly in emotional situations. "You need to be laughing and leaving, not staying and stewing" because the longer you stay in the problem situation, the higher the risk of acting irresponsible. <u>Get honest</u> (Block the thought)- Get honest with yourself about what will happen to your goals and feelings about yourself if you act on those unhealthy, harmful thoughts. Use "Fantasy fast forward" (p. 93) to play the tape in your head to the end consequences and tell yourself "I'm not falling into that". Tell yourself the truth that feelings can change over time but once you have done something, that can't be changed. If you can't deny the feeling, delay it by telling yourself "I can always do this tomorrow". <u>Get Responsible</u> (Substitute a more responsible thought)- Replace irresponsible thoughts (e.g., about eating, drinking, smoking, spending, cheating, hitting, cursing, stealing, getting sex, getting high, running away) with responsible thoughts. Begin by asking yourself, "How will that help me? or Why should I hurt me just because other people or other things hurt me?" Weigh your decision on the "Reality Scales" (below). [3]

List the last trouble you were involved in here: _____

Apply the steps to avoid that trouble if it occurs again and discuss this with your therapist or group if you are in treatment.

Get out: _____

Get honest: _____

_____

Get responsible: _____

_____

How to **C**alm down- The healthy behavior success skills used to calm down involves emotional control. These skills are often referred to as "emotional regulation" in treatment manuals. If you were standing next to your best friend when a problem situation hit you, they would show you concern by talking you down, not working you up. Unfortunately, we are not usually standing next to our best friend when problems hit. In these situations we have to learn to talk to ourselves like our own best friend. We have to talk ourselves down, not work ourselves up and help ourselves let go of unwanted feelings. We can do this by using the ABC's of letting feelings go as follows:

"A" is the Action that occurred (the problem situation or event); "B" is the Belief problem, about the action that works you up and triggers problem feelings or urges (i.e., often contains the word "should" or "must"); "C" is Challenging the Belief problem about the action in order to stop following the feeling and let it go.[3] For example: Action that occurred- Supervisor in a hurry raises their voice to you on in front of others; Belief problem- Telling yourself "They should respect me" triggers feeling frustrated and angry. This can result in having the last word and getting consequences if you can't let the feelings go and keep talking; Challenging the Belief problem- "Where is the evidence that people in a hurry, should slow down and lower their voice, I don't" and "How is me doing the wrong thing going to get them to do the right thing?" [4]

Think about the last time you got really upset. Apply the ABC's of letting feelings go to that situation and discuss it with your therapist or group if you are in treatment.

Action that occurred: _____

Belief problem: _____

_____

Challenging the belief problem: _____

_____

How to **T**hink it through- If you were ever asked "what were you thinking", chances are that you didn't think your decision through before you took action. Thinking it though by balancing the benefits against the drawbacks before making the decision is referred to as "decisional balance" in treatment manuals. Thinking it through is an important part of learning to talk to yourself like your own best friend. False friends who just want to be popular with everyone or people who want to stir up trouble, tell you what you want to hear. They help you minimize unhealthy, harmful behavior by using the words "just" and "only" (e.g., "It's a only little thing, no big deal" or "We'll just do it this one time"). Best friends are honest with you and tell you what you need to hear, not what you want to hear. If you were standing next to your best friend when you were hit with temptation to do something you shouldn't, they would give you a reality check. Your best friend would tell you that in reality, it's only a little thing if no harm can come to yourself or others and it's never just once. Since your best friend can't always be there to give you a reality check, you have to learn to do this yourself. The *reality check* and *reality scales* described below will help you weigh things out during difficult decisions, think it through and guide yourself into responsible action.

Use the Social Responsibility Check (reality check) for on the spot "snap" decisions by asking yourself "Is what I'm thinking about doing helpful or harmful to myself or others?" All decisions that could be harmful to self or others need to be weighted out further on three reality scales, the Survival Scale, the Success Scale and the Severity Scale. The Survival Scale evaluates how necessary for my survival it is to do the behavior being considered on a scale of zero (not necessary at all) to ten (absolutely necessary to save my life). Ask yourself, "How necessary for my survival is it for me to do what I am considering?" "What will happen to my survival if I don't act?" The Success Scale evaluates how important for my success is doing the responsible thing or failing to do it on a scale of zero (not important at all) to ten (so important that it could change the entire course of my life). Ask yourself, "How important is it to my success in life for me to do what I am considering?" "Do I have to do this in order to succeed in life?" The Severity (or Awful) Scale ("Bad Scale" for young children) evaluates how severe the consequences of doing the responsible thing or failing to do it will be on a scale of zero (not severe, awful or bad at all) to ten (so severe that I can't stand it, must avoid it and need help to overcome it). On one side of this scale is the reality of what will likely happen if the harmful behavior is committed. For example, "In the worst case, how severe could the consequences be if I smoked, drank or ate this and do I need to avoid these consequences?", "In the worst case, how severe could the consequences be if I took or smashed this and do I need to avoid these consequences?" or "In the worst case, how severe could the consequences be if I hit or fondled this person and do I need to avoid these consequences?" On the other side of this scale is the reality of what will likely happen if the harmful behavior is not committed. "How severe would the consequences be if I do the right thing and decide not to do this? Could I handle these consequences?" In summary, the severity scale is used to show concern for yourself and others by weighing out the severity of the consequences to yourself and others before taking action. [3]

List a recent decision mistake that you made: _____
Apply the Social Responsibility Check to that decision. My decision was (check one)...
__Helpful to me but harmful to others   __Harmful to me but helpful to others

__Helpful to myself and others   __Harmful to myself and others

List an important life decision that you need to make: _____
Use the Reality Scales to weigh out your decision and discuss this with your therapist or group if you are in treatment.

Survival scale rating ___(0- 10); Success scale rating ___(0- 10); Severity scale rating ___(0- 10)

My decision: _____

How to **S**olve the problem- Life always has problems that kick up feelings and require solutions. Behind every problem there is a goal. Problems are only problems when we are not meeting our goals to get what we want in life. The healthy behavior success skills used to solve the problems we face in life are referred to in treatment manuals as "social problem solving". Being able to "solve the problem" is needed to meet our goals to: get what we want; do as well as we want or; be treated the way we want in life. In order to get what you want in life, you need to get SET for solving problems in three steps: 1) Set your goal; 2) Evaluate your progress and options; 3) Take responsible action.

Set your goal involves getting honest with yourself about your goal. Ask yourself, What is my goal? What do I really want? Get honest about the problem and your real goal. Look at actual problem-solving goals not feelings about the problem. There is a big difference between solving the problem and just venting your feelings. For example, imagine you are a young person in a treatment program and your real goal is independence. You feel held back by adults because you are certain you can make it on your own if they just let you go. They keep reminding you that you haven't finished high school and believe you need more treatment to avoid relapse. You keep getting caught up in arguments over whether or not you can make it on your own.

Evaluate your progress and options. Evaluate your progress by asking yourself, "How well is what I am doing working in getting me what I want?" and "How will things likely to turn out for me if I continue this way?" This requires getting honest with yourself about your progress. For example, admitting that "Arguing over whether I can make it on my own if they just get out of my life is getting caught up in venting feelings, has not changed their minds and is not getting me any closer to actually being out on my own." Evaluate your options- Ask yourself, "What are my options?", "What can I change?", "What really needs to get done?" Make as long of a list as you can, be creative ask others for ideas. List all possible options and choices that could get you to your goal, then write it out for yourself. For example, "To be independent, I need my own place which takes money. My options are stealing, dealing, working going into the military or moving in with someone. I can change getting side-tracked in arguments on whether or not I can make it on my own, start really looking at what independence takes, 'keep my eyes on the prize', and figure out a way to get what I want. If I continue to vent my feelings over feeling held back without making a convincing plan to succeed, nothing will change. If I don't show them I know how to avoid relapse, I won't get out of treatment."

Take responsible action involves taking responsibility to change your method by getting honest with yourself about what needs to change and correcting your course. This involves answering the questions, "What do I need to do differently to reach my goal?", "What is the best way to get what I want?" and "What should I try first?" For example, "I need to do two things differently to reach my goal. First, I need to accept that reaching my goal will take more than just getting other people off my back and moving in with someone who will take care of me is not really making it on my own. In all honesty, I need a good job with health benefits or I need to get into the military. Both of these require graduating from high school and not relapsing back into another treatment program. Second, I need to stop letting my feelings get in the way of my goal to be on my own, stop arguing, start studying and finish treatment. I just got so mad when they told me 'you need to stop breeding and start reading' that I let my feelings get in the way of my goal. The best way to get what I want is to make the best relapse prevention plan I can. What I should try first is increased treatment participation and regular study hours." [3]

List a current problem that you are having: _____
Use the steps above to "solve the problem" and discuss this with your therapist or group if you are in treatment.

Set your goal: _____

Evaluate your progress and options: _____

_____

Take responsible action: _____

You can remember the healthy behavior success skills: **A**void trouble; **C**alm down; **T**hink it through and; **S**olve the problem by remembering that "actions speak louder than words" and thinking about your **ACTS**. Make a healthy relationship and behavior success skills cue card out of Table 2 below and carry it with you as a reminder of the skills you need to practice.

Table 2.
Healthy Behavior Success and Relationship Skills Cue Cards

Social Responsibility Therapy- Healthy <u>Relationship</u> Success Skills
What do we want from others in our life and what do they want from us?

Honesty- Involves getting honest <u>with yourself and others</u> by taking responsibility for mistakes and getting honest about others mistakes to keep them from getting in worse trouble later.

Trust- Involves <u>building trust</u> in others by keeping your word and respecting their feelings along with <u>learning to trust</u> others by opening up about problems and picking the right people to trust.

Loyalty- Involves <u>standing up for what you know is right</u> and who you know is right when there is peer pressure to keep quiet, "If you don't stand for something, you'll fall for anything."

Concern- Involves <u>helping self</u> by keeping personal problems "up front" so they don't get out of control again and <u>helping others</u> by treating others the way they want to be treated.

Responsibility- <u>Our number one responsibility is self-control</u>. Three others are emotional restitution (making things right), pulling our own weight and learning to accept feedback.

Social Responsibility Therapy- Healthy <u>Behavior</u> Success Skills

Avoid trouble (relapse prevention)- Use the 3-step social responsibility plan: <u>Get out</u> (Remove yourself)- "You need to be laughing and leaving, not staying and stewing"; <u>Get honest</u> (Block the thought)- Tell yourself the truth, feelings change but actions can't be changed. If you can't deny the feeling delay it. Tell yourself "I can always do this tomorrow". <u>Get Responsible</u> (Substitute a more responsible thought)- Weigh your decision on the "Reality Scales".

Calm down (emotional regulation)- The ABC's of letting feelings go: "A" is the <u>Action that occurred</u>; "B" is the <u>Belief problem</u>, i.e., the word "should" or "must" that is triggering the feeling; "C" is <u>Challenging the Belief problem</u> in order to stop following the feeling and let it go (See Ellis & Bernard, 2006; Ellis & Velten, 1992).

Think it through (decisional balance)- Involves a Social Responsibility Check- "Is what I'm considering helpful/harmful to myself and others?" and three <u>Reality Scales</u> (0 to 10 scales):
Survival scale- How important to my survival is it for me to...
Success scale- How important for my success is it for me to...
Severity scale (Bad or Awful scale)- How severe would the consequences be if I...

Solve the problem (social problem solving)- Get <u>SET</u> for solving problems: 1) <u>S</u>et your goal; 2) <u>E</u>valuate your progress and options; 3) <u>T</u>ake responsible action.

The Problem Development Triad: How Harmful Behavior was Acquired- The Risk Factor Chain

"Those who cannot remember the past are condemned to repeat it" -- George Santayana [5]

Understanding How Harmful Behavior was Acquired: The Risk Factor Chain

No one just got up one morning and said "It's raining outside, I think I'll stay inside and start developing a harmful behavior problem". It wasn't a snap decision and maybe not a decision at all. It developed over a period of time through a Risk Factor Chain that Led up to that harmful behavior problem which involved the following five links. This first workbook in the Social Responsibility Therapy series focuses on developing an understanding how harmful behavior was acquired through the Risk Factor Chain (i.e., Section 1 of The Problem Development Triad).

In the Risk Factor Chain, Link 1 Historical Risk Factors consists of stressful life experiences such as toxic parenting, abuse, neglect or other traumatic events that lead to feeling ineffective, powerless or helpless which stunts personal growth. This sets the occasion for Link 2 Social-Emotional Risk Factors such as lying to avoid consequences and emotional maturity problems such as dwelling on or always thinking about past injustices or mistreatment which creates unwanted feelings. Social-emotional problems leave a person feeling one down and gravitates them towards Link 3 Situational Risk Factors (i.e., high risk situations where they have access to relapse activities such as smoking, drinking, drugging or overeating) and feel less insecure (e.g., are around negative peers) or more in control (e.g., are around those they can influence). Link 4 Cognitive Risk Factors is the last link to relapse which involves Irresponsible Thinking excuses to do what you want and reasons why it is OK. Being in Link 3 high risk situations for relapse with a Link 1 life stress history and Link 2 social-emotional problems requires only minimal Link 4 irresponsible thinking to trigger Link 5 unhealthy, behavior.

The Risk Factor Chain which starts with having problems and ends up with acting those problems out, can stunt social-emotional growth to the point where serious self-control problems and difficulty with all forms of relationships are created. This portion of your Social Responsibility Therapy will help you understand the Risk Factor Chain that helped you acquire or start your harmful behavior. Understanding how you got your problem to begin with is very important if you want to avoid repeating it or developing a new type of harmful behavior after you have completed your treatment for your present one. Understanding the links in the chain which led up to your harmful behavior, you will help you identify issues that need to be dealt with in order to help maintain your recovery. A Summary of the Risk Factor Chain that led to your harmful behavior is provided on the following page (see Figure 3, p. 18).

What's in it for me? Understanding what leads up to harmful behavior is extremely important if you want to avoid developing a new harmful behavior after you have completed treatment. However, with self-help workbooks as well as group, family and individual therapy...
"You only get out of it, what you put into it" (Greg Norman and many before him) which basically means that a self-help workbook is only as good as the honesty of the person completing it. The more honest you are, the more self-knowledge you will develop. This is

critically important because knowledge is power, self-knowledge is self-control power and self-control is the key to your future success.

Figure 3.
How Harmful Behavior was Acquired: The Risk Factor Chain
(that led to harmful behavior, i.e., biopsychosocial risk factors)

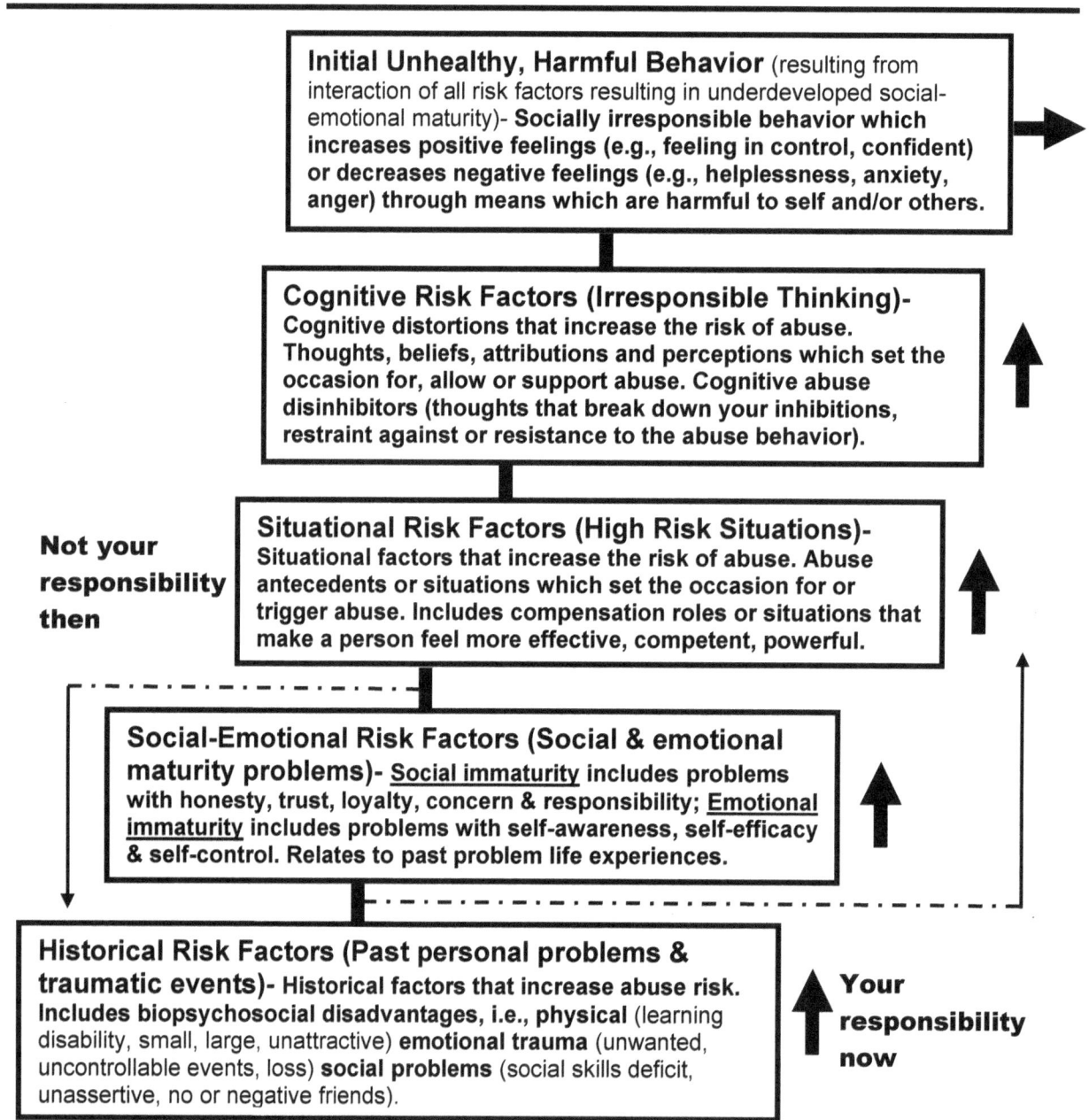

Initial Unhealthy, Harmful Behavior (resulting from interaction of all risk factors resulting in underdeveloped social-emotional maturity)- **Socially irresponsible behavior which increases positive feelings (e.g., feeling in control, confident) or decreases negative feelings (e.g., helplessness, anxiety, anger) through means which are harmful to self and/or others.**

Cognitive Risk Factors (Irresponsible Thinking)- **Cognitive distortions that increase the risk of abuse. Thoughts, beliefs, attributions and perceptions which set the occasion for, allow or support abuse. Cognitive abuse disinhibitors (thoughts that break down your inhibitions, restraint against or resistance to the abuse behavior).**

Not your responsibility then

Situational Risk Factors (High Risk Situations)- **Situational factors that increase the risk of abuse. Abuse antecedents or situations which set the occasion for or trigger abuse. Includes compensation roles or situations that make a person feel more effective, competent, powerful.**

Social-Emotional Risk Factors (Social & emotional maturity problems)- Social immaturity **includes problems with honesty, trust, loyalty, concern & responsibility;** Emotional immaturity **includes problems with self-awareness, self-efficacy & self-control. Relates to past problem life experiences.**

Historical Risk Factors (Past personal problems & traumatic events)- **Historical factors that increase abuse risk. Includes biopsychosocial disadvantages, i.e., physical** (learning disability, small, large, unattractive) **emotional trauma** (unwanted, uncontrollable events, loss) **social problems** (social skills deficit, unassertive, no or negative friends).

Your responsibility now

Note: Management of these risk factors is summarized in Exhibit 1 (p. 84).

The Risk Factor Chain: LINK #1- Historical Risk Factors
(Past personal problems)

"That which does not kill us makes us stronger."-- Friedrich Nietzsche (1844- 1900)

Name _____   **Date** _____

Definition: Historical Risk Factors involve past personal problems (i.e., past traumatic events or things that created permanent problems) that increase the risk of harmful behavior. In other words, these are harmful things that happened to you that set you up for doing harmful things to yourself or others. These past personal problems often involve biopsychosocial problems and past situations that have had a lasting or permanent effect. Biopsychosocial problems involve biological, psychological and social problems that you have. Biological problems are physical in nature, relate to the body and are often inherited from parents (e.g., being small, large, short, tall, thin, overweight, unattractive, having a physical disability or learning disability) or brain biochemistry problems resulting in unwanted feelings (e.g., problems such depression, anxiety, anger, mood swings). Psychological problems are often emotional in nature and relate to emotional trauma such as uncontrollable past abuse or loss resulting in unwanted feelings (e.g., anger, anxiety, depression, helplessness) and associated thoughts (e.g., about injustices, consequences, past abuse, not being able to do things). Social problems are often skills-based in nature and relate to problem interactions with others such as having a social skills deficit, being unassertive, shy, having no friends or having negative friends which can impact achievement and employment.

Risk Factor Question #1: What difficult times and harmful situations you have experienced in the past?

Use the space below to write your a first draft of your "Life Story" that covers the past personal problems, issues and upsetting things that you have had to deal with during your life. Write the story with a beginning, middle and end. Begin by introducing yourself with your name, age, where you were born and lived. Start with the first memory you have of problems, conflicts or issues. If you can't remember dates, use places. For example, "When I was in elementary school..." End by connecting what happened in your past to where you are now (your present problems). For example, "My past issues left me thinking... feeling... resulted in treatment for..."

My life story and past problem history- _____

_____

_____

_____

_____

_____

_____

Now that you have finished your first draft, complete the following sections A- G to help jog your memory about some of the things you may have experienced in the past but forgotten.

A. Please check all of the UPSETTING THINGS that have <u>happened to you</u> or your family WHEN you were growing up.

___ Parent divorce (How many?___) or ___ parent separation (How many?___)

___ Parent had partners that I had conflicts with or didn't like

___ Having acne or not feeling attractive

___ Being made fun of by other students a lot

___ Feeling bad about being (__ over or __ under) weight or being called "fat" or "skinny"

___ Feeling bad about being too (__ short or __ tall) or being called "shrimp" or "bean pole"

___ Feeling like I didn't fit in: __not having friends; __not being popular; __ being picked on

___ Getting poor grades in school or having learning problems, being put in a special class, having a tutor or always being the last person to turn things in

___ Feeling socially uncomfortable, not easily able to come up and talk to people or shy

___ Not being good at anything like sports, music/school band, video games, skate boarding etc.

___ Getting sexual feelings but not confident enough to ask someone my age to go out with me

___ Being afraid of rejection by people my age and realizing that younger children accept me

___ Hanging out with those who get in trouble

___ Parent or primary caretaker (relative or adult you lived with) had alcoholic/drug problem

___ Parent or primary caretaker has been in therapy over one year or in a psychiatric hospital

___ Parent or primary caretaker has been in jail or charged with a crime by the court or welfare department

___ Always an uproar or conflict at home

___ Witnessed or saw: (__physical, __emotional, __sexual) abuse in the family

(Who did it? _____)

___ Introduced to watching sex videos (before you were 12)

___ Introduced to drugs/alcohol by a parent or older sibling

___ Watching adults or parents having sexual contact (more than just kissing)

___ Adults would argue over my discipline in front of me

___ My supervision was: __too lax (I didn't get checked on); __too strict (I couldn't do anything)

___ My discipline was: __too lax (few consequences); __too strict (severe consequences)

___My discipline was based on feelings. If my (__mother; __father; __primary caretaker) was feeling good, I wouldn't get consequences, if they were upset, I would really get it

Please check all of the UPSETTING THINGS that have <u>happened to you</u> or your family WHEN you were growing up.

___I got few consequences for my behavior with brothers or sisters but severe consequences for problems that upset my (__mother; __father; __primary caretaker)

___ One parent/guardian would often show that they felt sorry for me or let me off of a discipline given by the other

___ At least one parent/caretaker always criticizing me or never told me when I did good

___ One of the other children in the family was the favorite and got more attention, privileges and less discipline

___ Emotionally distant (__mother; __ father; __caretaker) who was never involved with me

___ Parent/caretaker treated me like a friend not a child, told me adult problems, leaned on me

___ Parent/caretaker didn't run things, put me in a position where I more or less had to act like a parent and be responsible for taking care of things

___ Over-controlling parent/caretaker who really dominated my every move (List _____)

___ Over-protective parent/caretaker who blamed others for my mistakes (List _____)

___ I never really felt love, true concern or cared for by my (__ mother; __father; __caretaker)

___ I felt like my (__mother; __father; __caretaker) was ashamed of me, disappointed in me or I didn't measure up to what they wanted

___ The only time I remember being sat down and talked to by a parent was after I got in trouble

___ Absent father or father figure (__died, __left family or __never present, gone a lot)

___ Absent mother or mother figure (__died, __left family or __never present, gone a lot)

___ Father or father figure present physically but not there for me, always into something else

___ Mother or mother figure present physically but not there for me, always into something else

___ Family experienced repeated or ongoing problems with (check): __unemployment; __money

___ I moved more than once (How many moves? ___)

___ I (check): __ was adopted; __experienced a failed adoption

___ I had more than one change in caretakers (How many? ___)

___ I was placed on probation/parole (How many times? ___)

___ I was placed in a: __foster home (How many? ___); __group home (How many? ___)

___ I was placed in a special education class for: __learning problems; __behavior problems

___ I was placed in detention center (How many times? ___)

___ I was placed in a residential treatment center (How many times? ___)

Please check all of the UPSETTING THINGS that have <u>happened to you</u> or your family WHEN you were growing up.

___ I was placed in drug/alcohol treatment (How many times? ___; Overdoses?___)

___ My house was too crowded, I slept with more than one other child or never had any privacy

___ Lived with more than one male caretaker (e.g., dad, step/foster dad) How many? ___

___ Lived with more than one female caretaker (e.g., mom, step/foster mom) How many? ___

___ I was a teenage parent (How many children? ___)

___ I was in a psychiatric hospital (How many times? ___; Suicidal?___)

___ I have received traumatic injuries (__shot, __stabbed, __beaten, __hospitalized for injuries)

___ I was in a general hospital for a head injury or injuries which included a head injury

___ I had a selfish (__mother; __ father; __caretaker) that got annoyed whenever I wanted them to do something with me. I felt resented like I was getting in the way of their life.

___ I was __overactive, __overly self-conscious, __overly sensitive (easily hurt, easily startled)

___too responsible (Felt if I just do better trouble will stop OR had to care for other children)

___I think I needed counseling for _____ but didn't get it.

B. Please check all of the UPSETTING THINGS that have <u>happened to you</u> AT ANY TIME in your life.

___ I have had more than a few serious relationship break ups.

___ I have had fairly serious relationship problems

___ I have been arrested.

___ I have been in counseling for family problems.

___ I have been in counseling for emotional problems (i.e., problems with feelings such as depression, anxiety or anger).

___ I have had children removed from my home (placed in detention, foster care, adoption)

___ I have been separated or divorced.

___ I have been in counseling for relationship problems

___ I have had probation/parole violations.

___ I have been in counseling for behavior problems.

___ I have been in counseling for drug/alcohol problems.

___ I have received psychiatric medications

___ I was in a psychiatric hospital (How many times? ___; Suicidal? ___)

C. Please record all other hurtful or harmful events that you experienced.
Write what happened below. Include any loss of individuals close to you that really hurt.

_____

_____

_____

_____

(If you need more space, use the workspace on page 79, 116 or the inside of the front and back covers)

D. Please list total number of upsetting things that happened to you.

Count up everything you checked in Section A, B and C and list that here.
On questions that asked "How many" count one for each time you listed _____

E. Review the following list of HARMFUL, DESTRUCTIVE THINGS that may have caused emotional wounds and set the occasion for or led to a lack of self-efficacy (confidence) and/or social-emotional maturity problems. Read each statement carefully.

If you **have experienced the harmful behavior** described **rate how harmful** it was to you.

0 Not Harmful to me at all	1 A little Harmful	2 Moderately Harmful	3 Highly Harmful	4 Extremely Harmful

____ 1) An absent mother (i.e., a mother who was not in the home)?

What was her absence due to? ___ running away/abandoning family; ___ divorce;

___ never marrying father; ___ death; ___ suicide; ___ military service; ___ prison/jail;

___ job related travel; ___ drug/alcohol treatment; ___ psychiatric hospitalization.

____ 2) An absent father (i.e., a father who was not in the home)?

What was his absence due to? ___ running away/abandoning family; ___ divorce;

___ never marrying mother; ___ death; ___ suicide; ___ military service; ___ prison/jail;

___ job related travel; ___ drug/alcohol treatment; ___ psychiatric hospitalization.

____ 3) Trust abuse (e.g., lying or continually breaking promises, regularly making plans that are not carried out)? Who did this to you? (check as many as needed):

___ mother; ___ father; ___ step-mother; ___ step-father; ___ girlfriend; ___ boyfriend;

___ close friend; ___ school mate; ___ coworker ___ other (list here- _____).

____ 4) Emotional abuse (everything had to be perfect but there were no threats of physical violence)- Severely judgmental, critical and perfectionist parent. Whatever you did, it wasn't good enough. Always put down, picked on or criticized without clear explanation of what was done wrong. Parent threats to throw you out of the house or being a rageaholic (i.e., going off and constantly yelling while calling you names) and putting you down for no apparent reason other than getting angry or upset. For example "you dumb ass, I hate you and wish you were dead!" Who did this to you? (check as many as needed):

___ mother; ___ father; ___ step-mother; ___ step-father; ___ girlfriend; ___ boyfriend;

___ close friend; ___ school mate; ___ coworker ___ other (list here- _____).

____ 5) Verbal abuse or menacing (i.e., serious threats to harm you physically). Who did this to you? (check as many as needed):

___ mother; ___ father; ___ step-mother; ___ step-father; ___ girlfriend; ___ boyfriend;

___ close friend; ___ school mate; ___ coworker ___ other (list here- _____).

If you **have experienced the harmful behavior** described **rate how harmful** it was to you.

0 Not Harmful to me at all	1 A little Harmful	2 Moderately Harmful	3 Highly Harmful	4 Extremely Harmful

___ 6) Power abuse (e.g., giving no choices, controlling your every move, allowing no personal freedom, always over-reacting, demanding that you completely control your facial expression, tone of voice and body language when around them orders or acting jealous of your friends)? Who did this to you? (check as many as needed):

___ mother; ___ father; ___ step-mother; ___ step-father; ___ girlfriend; ___ boyfriend;

___ close friend; ___ school mate; ___ coworker ___ other (list here- _____).

___ 7) Emotional neglect (e.g., being around physically but not being there for you emotionally. For example, being a workaholic, a couch potato T.V. addict, being obsessed with hobbies or sports, being depressed, extremely selfish or caring more about drugs/alcohol)? Who did this to you? (check as many as needed):

___ mother; ___ father; ___ step-mother; ___ step-father; ___ girlfriend; ___ boyfriend;

___ close friend; ___ school mate; ___ coworker ___ other (list here- _____).

___ 8) Physical neglect (e.g., parents not providing you with three good meals a day, not getting you the clothes, shoes or school supplies you need, not giving you a place where you can sleep without being disturbed, not asking about or caring where you go or what you do including things which are not good for you like staying out all night, drinking, etc.)? Which parent(s) did this to you? (check as many as needed):
___ mother; ___ father; ___ step-mother; ___ step-father; ___ other (list-_____).

___ 9) Physical abuse or assault (e.g., beatings or any punishment which left bruises, welts or scars including ongoing school bullying)? Who did this to you? (check as many as needed):

___ mother; ___ father; ___ step-mother; ___ step-father; ___ girlfriend; ___ boyfriend;

___ close friend; ___ school mate; ___ coworker ___ other (list here- _____).

___ 10) Sexual abuse (i.e., any touching or sexual advance on you by another person without your consent)? Who did this to you? (check as many as needed):

___ mother; ___ father; ___ step-mother; ___ step-father; ___ girlfriend; ___ boyfriend;

___ close friend; ___ school mate; ___ coworker ___ other (list here- _____).

F. Link #1- Past Personal Problems Summary

1) Review the Past Personal Problems that you have experienced and list the top three harmful, upsetting things that happened to you from sections A through E above (i.e., the ones that you rated the highest on pages 21- 25).

Most upsetting thing that happened to me _____

2nd most upsetting thing _____

3rd most upsetting thing _____

What were you **thinking** when these things were happening? (Hint: If you are not sure what you were thinking and need some ideas to jog your memory, read Appendix C., page 94)

_____

What were you **feeling** when these things were happening? _____

_____

G. Link #1 Summary Completion Instructions- Record at least your top 3 Past Personal Problems (i.e., the most upsetting things you listed in section F) that had the most significant effect on your life and set the occasion for social and emotional problems **on your Risk Factor Chain worksheet (page 81)** at the end of this section (use the second page "continued" portion of your worksheet if needed). Imagine yourself teaching someone else about this part of your life. Put your important descriptions in phrase form that makes it easy for you to explain and makes sense when read by others. Don't limit yourself to the top three points if there are important parts that fit in this area. Make sure that you do not leave out any important information about yourself on this topic. Use the margins if needed.

Now return to "My life story" (p. 19- 20) and update it. Add the important things you checked in sections A- G to your first draft. Review page 11 and be sure to add how these past events effected your honesty, trust, loyalty, concern and responsibility. Talk with a counselor about the effect that these things had on you, how they influenced your life and what you can do about it. This section reviewed the past and other people's behavior which are the only two things that you can't change in life. Since thinking about things you can't change can make you feel helpless, use the space below to show how you can use the ABC's of letting feelings go (page 12- 13) to "calm down" when you get upset. Discuss the dangers of going over and over problems about the past or other people's behavior and what you need to do about it (Hint: See Link #1, page 84).

Action that occurred: _____

Belief problem: _____

_____

Challenging the belief problem: _____

_____

(If you need more space, use the workspace on page 79, 116 or the inside of the front and back covers)

Get honest about your Past Personal Problems. Discuss your life story with your therapist or group if you are in treatment. If you are in a treatment group, read it to the group. Getting honest with yourself on the questions in this section will build the self-awareness needed to help you avoid relapse but it won't provide relief or recommendations from others. The saying "The truth will set you free" only applies if you have the courage to get it out and ask for help.

Log the date you discussed these issues and who you discussed them with below.

Date: _____ Discussed with: _____

The Risk Factor Chain: LINK #2- Social-Emotional Risk Factors
(Social-Emotional Maturity Problems)

"Maturity is achieved when a person postpones immediate pleasures for long-term values."-- Joshua L. Liebman

Name: _____   **Date:** _____

Definition: Social-Emotional Risk Factors involve problems with both Social and Emotional Maturity.

Social Maturity involves the healthy development of honesty, trust, loyalty, concern and responsibility. Many Social Maturity Problems may have a connection to Historical Risk Factors. For example, the Social Maturity Problem of dishonesty about mistakes may have been used to avoid abusive consequences. Learning that dishonesty works in avoiding abusive consequences interferes with learning to value honesty. In this case, the person may have difficulty coming to understand that honesty is needed to build trust. They may view trust as something they are entitled to like a legal right. If they apply the legal view that you are "innocent until proven guilty" to trust they will believe "they should trust me until they see a problem or I do something wrong". This interferes with understanding that trust is something that has to be earned and is part of a developing relationship. In reality, people don't trust you until you earn it by being responsible or they get to know you well enough to trust you. Another social maturity problem that individuals with a history of abuse can easily get is distrusting others. Distrust can lead to testing people by acting out and feeling they "should" make up for the past hurt from others by having extra patience with them when their behavior deserves consequences. This irresponsible belief creates serious relationship problems particularly with authorities. In addition, current problems with loyalty to others may have a connection with past childhood physical, emotional or sexual abuse that helped develop an "Every man for himself" survival attitude towards others. That attitude interferes with valuing family loyalty and learning the social responsibility to "be your brother's keeper". Individuals with behavior that is primarily harmful to self may be overly trustworthy and loyal, getting involved too quickly and remaining in relationships with others who are not dependable. They may have more concern for others than they do for themselves, take on too much responsibility and blame themselves unnecessarily. Individuals with behavior that is primarily harmful to others may have problems being trustworthy since they don't feel others can be trusted resulting in attachment problems with others and a lack of relationship commitment or loyalty. They may care more about themselves, be less responsible to others and blame them for their problems. In all cases, the need to address honesty, trust, loyalty, concern, and responsibility is clear, though the direction of development (e.g., increase versus decrease or toward self versus others) may be different. Confidence is built on identity (knowing who you are). Who you are is what you stand for so you need to stand for something (See Link #2, p. 84).

Emotional Maturity involves the healthy development of self-awareness, self-efficacy (confidence) and self-control. Emotional maturity issues also often have connections to Historical Risk Factors. For example, automatic denial of problems for fear of consequences or automatic denial feelings for fear of exposing weakness in the past can become a habit leading to automatic denial of minor mistakes and feelings in the present. Automatic denial reactions which are done without thinking are behavior habits done without self-awareness of motivations and feelings. Abusive parenting may lead to actually believing that some of the statements that were said in anger by parents are actually true. This belief can lead to low self-efficacy, a lack of confidence, not believing in yourself or feeling inferior (i.e., not as good as others). Believing that the hurt is deserved can lead to feeling helpless and ruminating (i.e., going over and over) about injustices. This can turn depression into anger and increase the chances of acting feelings out. "Hanging with negative inferiors" is one way that people make up for feeling inferior, not as good as others or one down. Hanging out with (or comparing yourself with) people who are worse than you can make you feel OK or even one up from them. Associating with negative others while upset or angry decreases self-control and increases the probability of getting involved in harmful behavior. Emotional immaturity is associated with self-defeating habits such as an exaggerated need for acceptance, excitement and attention along with justifying actions based on feelings.

Self-awareness involves "knowing where you are coming from" emotionally. This means being aware of your feelings, what triggered them and understanding the emotional motivation for what you said or did. For example, "I got angry after they ignored me which is why I ended up yelling at them". Problems with self-awareness include not being in touch with feelings when they occur and not realizing what you are saying to yourself that results in you saying or doing something. Self-awareness can be blocked by repeated past abuse which can throw a person into automatic "fight or flight" mode where they learn to do things automatically on instinct without self-awareness and thinking it through. Emotions can shut down self-awareness. For example, being overwhelmed by anxiety can block out awareness of your surroundings and give you "tunnel vision". Flying into a rage can block out hearing important things that are being said to you. A lack of foresight or mental ability to plan ahead is a self-awareness problem known as a "foresight deficit decision" that allows you to slip strait into trouble (see Appendix B examples, p. 90). Self-awareness is built up by adopting the "Mirror Concept" and learning to use others feedback as a mirror to see yourself in order to become more self-aware.

Self-efficacy is confidence that you can be effective and do things. Self-efficacy is your self-effectiveness belief that "I can do it", that you have the power to be effective, master or change things. It is the opposite of the "I can't" belief that triggers feeling helpless. Problems with self-efficacy include feeling ineffective, incompetent, helpless and experiencing a control and power loss. Self-efficacy is torn down by focusing on things that you can't control like the past and other people's behavior. This includes the negative, upsetting, uncontrollable experiences that you listed as your Historical Risk Factors in Link one of your Risk Factor Chain. Self-efficacy is built up by focusing on things you can control like the present and your behavior. This includes positive, rewarding experiences such as: mastery of mental skills like figuring out how to fix something or feeling good about doing well on a school test; mastery of physical behavior skills like feeling good about doing something well in a baseball game and; mastery of social skills like being able to do and say the right things to make friends and get yourself involved in activities with others. The old saying that "nothing succeeds like success" applies to building self-efficacy because the more things you try, the more successful experiences you can have and the more confident you can feel in your ability to succeed. In building self-efficacy, you have to try things to build confidence, not wait for the confidence to try things.

Self-control is our number one social responsibility. We owe it to ourselves to practice self-control in order to avoid unwanted consequences and we owe it to others as a social responsibility to treat others as we want to be treated. Self-control is where social maturity and emotional maturity overlap since self-control is our number one responsibility and responsibility is a key component in social maturity. Problems with self-control involves taking actions based on unverified assumptions or emotional state which results in socially irresponsible behavior including over reactions and actions that were unnecessary. Self-control is worn down by drugs and alcohol. There is a strong link between getting high and getting in trouble. The saying that "the superego is soluble in alcohol and evaporates with drugs" reminds us that that our sense of right and wrong along with our ability to think about consequences dissolves when we get high. Strong emotions can also get in the way of self control. Justifying actions (i.e., harmful behavior) based on feelings anger, anxiety and depression is common. Domestic violence arrests often result from justifying the action of hitting a partner based on feelings of anger. Running from treatment programs after making a mistake is often justified by anxiety/fear over getting consequences for that mistake. Suicide attempts often result from justifying giving up on life based on feelings of depression (i.e., that things are hopeless and won't get better). Negative peer influence can also decrease self-control. This is where understanding your needs is very important. Everyone has needs for acceptance, attention and excitement. Nobody wants to be rejected, ignored or bored. Sometimes we go along to get along, be accepted and not make waves. Sometimes we compromise ourselves, what we know is right or what we feel comfortable with to be accepted. Other times we do things for the attention we will get or the excitement that goes with it. Sometimes it's a combination. For example, thrill crimes like shoplifting with peers can involve attention, acceptance and excitement. Negative peer influence is a strong factor in returning to harmful behavior. Just like math where a negative number multiplied by a negative number is a positive number, in social contacts a negative person hanging with another a negative person is positive for trouble. Self-control can also be broken down by ruminating (i.e., going over and over) on past injustices which leads to keeping score, getting even and taking out feelings on others.

While abusive parenting in Link 1 of the Risk Factor Chain may push individuals away from family, Link 2 social-emotional problems may pull individuals towards negative peers. This can occur when individuals don't feel like they fit in with positive peers and begin to associate with negative peers who are less threatening and more likely to accept them. The down side here is "When in Rome do as the Romans do" which means being willing to do things that are wrong or risky with these peers in order to be accepted and fit in with them. In addition, feeling insecure, inadequate or rejected from family (either by parent neglect or absence/workaholism) makes it more important to want to be accepted by peers giving peers a stronger influence on self-control.

Risk Factor Question #2: What about your past experiences may have affected your social and emotional maturity?

A. Social Maturity: Review your Link 1 Summary in the previous section (page 25- 26). Think about how the top three upsetting things, past hurt or trauma have affected you and mark your feelings on the graphs below.

Use the numbers on the scale below to rate the following statements about yourself.

0	1	2	3	4
Never	Sometimes	Half of the time	Often	Almost Always

____ 1) Been too honest and open, had problems with telling too much to others too soon.

Use the numbers on the scale below to rate the following statements about yourself.

0	1	2	3	4
Never	Sometimes	Half of the time	Often	Almost Always

____ 2) Was not honest about my problems and pretended things were OK when they weren't.

____ 3) Been too guarded and closed, always keeping secrets about problems.

____ 4) Had times in my life when lying became an issue.

____ 5) Lied or left things out to help myself or avoid consequences.

____ 6) Lied or misled others to get even, hurt them or get them consequences.

____ 7) Been too trustworthy and got involved too quickly in relationships.

____ 8) Got upset because I thought people should give me a chance, trust me and only start checking on me if I mess up.

____ 9) Distrusted people expecting them to be like others who I couldn't trust in the past.

____ 10) Thinking others can't be trusted in relationships and checking on them

____ 11) Had times in my life when I couldn't trust myself to do the right thing.

____ 12) Had times when I couldn't be trusted by others.

____ 13) Been too loyal and stayed with others who are not dependable.

____ 14) Bailed out of relationships too soon or kept old relationships going.

____ 15) Put friends before family including being there for them and giving more to them.

____ 16) Had times in my life when I wasn't loyal to others in relationships and cheated.

____ 17) Held the attitude of "It's every man for himself" and said or done what was best for me which was no doubt not best for the other person.

____ 18) Had times in my life when I showed more concern for others than I did for myself.

____ 19) Had times in my life when I didn't care about myself or what happened to me.

____ 20) Thought people close to me who knew what I've been through should show me some concern and cut me some slack.

____ 21) Had times in my life when I showed more concern for myself than I did for others.

____ 22) Had times in my life when I didn't care about others or their feelings.

____ 23) Told myself, "You have to look out for number one" and made decisions without considering what could happen to others.

____ 24) Been overly responsible and tried to do everything just right.

____ 25) Viewed by others as someone who can be counted on to do my part and get things done.

Use the numbers on the scale below to rate the following statements about yourself.

0	1	2	3	4
Never	Sometimes	Half of the time	Often	Almost Always

___ 26) Overloaded myself by doing too much for others.

___ 27) Put more into relationships than I got out of them.

___ 28) Had times when I took too much of the blame for relationship or family problems.

___ 29) Been irresponsible and let things go.

___ 30) Had times in my life when I couldn't be counted on to get things done.

___ 31) Overloaded others by not doing my part

___ 32) Took more from relationships than I put into them.

___ 33) Had times in my life when I didn't take enough responsibility for my part in problems

___ 34) Had times when I blamed others for things that were my responsibility.

___ 35) Had times when I blamed others for my behavior or my part in problems, for example saying they shouldn't have gotten me started

B. Self-Awareness: Review your Link 1 Summary on the previous page. Think about how the top three <u>upsetting things, past hurt or trauma have left you feeling</u> and mark your feelings on the graphs below. See "Basic Human Emotions: 101" on page 43 for explanation.

Use the numbers on the scale below to <u>rate how the top three upsetting things, past hurt or trauma that you experienced has left you feeling</u>. If not all of the capitalized words apply to you, underline the ones that do apply and cross out the ones that don't before you rate each item.

0	1	2	3	4
Not at all	A Little	Moderately	Highly	Extremely

___ 1) How generally ANGRY, HOSTILE and HATEFUL these things have left you feeling.

___ 2) How generally FRUSTRATED, RESENTFUL and WANTING TO GET EVEN OR STRIKE OUT these things have left you feeling.

___ 3) How generally BITTER AND MISERABLE these things have left you feeling.

___ 4) How generally LET DOWN and DISAPPOINTED these things have left you feeling.

___ 5) How generally INADEQUATE, LIKE A FAILURE OR LIKE NOTHING I COULD DO WAS RIGHT these things have left you feeling.

___ 6) How generally INEFFECTIVE, HELPLESS and POWERLESS these things have left you feeling.

___ 7) How generally SAD and DEPRESSED these things have left you feeling.

Use the numbers on the scale below to <u>rate how the top three upsetting things, past hurt or trauma that you experienced has left you feeling.</u> If not all of the capitalized words apply to you, underline the ones that do apply and cross out the ones that don't before you rate each item.

0	1	2	3	4
Not at all	A Little	Moderately	Highly	Extremely

___ 8) How generally REJECTED and HURT these things have left you feeling.

___ 9) How generally GUILTY and BLAMING MYSELF these things have left you feeling.

___ 10) How generally EMBARRASSED and ASHAMED these things have left you feeling.

___ 11) How generally DISGUSTED and FILTHY these things have left you feeling.

___ 12) How generally LONELY AND NOT UNDERSTOOD these things have left you feeling.

___ 13) How generally MIXED UP and CONFUSED these things have left you feeling.

___ 14) How generally FEARFUL, ANXIOUS and TENSE these things have left you feeling.

Demonstrate your self-awareness by completing the following sentences about yourself

People view me as _____

I get angry about _____

I like to _____

My biggest goal is _____

I am ashamed of _____

I am good at _____

I have wanted to _____

I get embarrassed by _____

Someday I would like to _____

I think school/work _____

I get anxious about _____

My friends _____

I would like to be known for _____

My strength is _____

I get sad about _____

My weakness is _____

I have wished that _____

I think a lot about _____

When upset, I usually feel _____

I do unhealthy, harmful behavior when _____

To get the healthy body I want, I need to_____

To get the healthy relationships I want, I need to_____

To get the healthy life direction I want, I need to_____

C. Self-Efficacy (confidence): Review the section above to get back in touch with how the top three <u>upsetting things, past hurt or trauma that you listed on your Link #1 summary have left you feeling</u>. Think about the ways that the feelings that you marked above have affected your life and made it difficult for you to master, do or try things.

Use the numbers on the scale below to **rate how serious your confidence problems have been** when trying to master mental tasks, behaviors or social things.

0 Not at all	1 Somewhat	2 Moderately	3 Highly	4 Extremely

___ 1) How serious have your confidence problems been when trying to master **mental tasks** (for example schoolwork, homework or other forms of learning)?

<u>**Mental** tasks I haven't tried to do or master</u> (or started but then quit before I could do it well)

_____

_____

_____

Thoughts or feelings that stopped me from trying to do or master these mental tasks.

_____

_____

_____

Use the numbers on the scale below to **rate how serious your confidence problems have been** when trying to master physical tasks.

0 Not at all	1 Somewhat	2 Moderately	3 Highly	4 Extremely

___ 2) How serious have your confidence problems been when trying to master **physical behaviors** (for example a specific sport or musical instrument you liked)?

<u>**Physical** behaviors I haven't tried to do or master</u> (or started but quit before I could do well)

_____

_____

_____

Thoughts or feelings that stopped me from trying to do or master these physical behaviors.

_____

_____

_____

Use the numbers on the scale below to **rate how serious your confidence problems have been** when trying to master social things.

0	1	2	3	4
Never	**Sometimes**	**Half of the time**	**Often**	**Almost Always**

___ 3) How serious have your confidence problems been when trying to master **social activities** (for example asking someone out on a date, going to parties, trying out for a play)?

<u>**Social** activities I haven't tried to do or master</u> (or started but quit before I could do it well)

_____

_____

_____

Thoughts or feelings that stopped me from trying to do or these social activities.

_____

_____

_____

Use the numbers on the scale below to rate how the upsetting, harmful things that happened to you in your life affected you.

0	1	2	3	4
Never	**Sometimes**	**Half of the time**	**Often**	**Almost Always**

The upsetting, harmful things that happened to me in my life...

___ 4) left me feeling like a failure, that I had something to prove and thinking about showing everyone I could make it.

___ 5) left me feeling unaccepted, not confident around others and made it more important for me to get acceptance from others.

___ 6) included not getting much adult attention for trying new things or doing well which left me feeling ignored, afraid to try things and wanting peer attention.

___ 7) left me not knowing how to handle boredom and being used to family fighting, drama or something always going on made it important for me to be doing something exciting.

___ 8) left me feeling like I will never be able to do anything right so why even try.

____ 9) included hurtful, rejecting things that made it more important for me to be accepted and got me saying too much to others too soon in trying to be accepted.

____ 10) helped me give up on trying to tell the truth or explain myself and just lie.

Use the numbers on the scale below to rate how the upsetting, harmful things that happened to you in your life affected you.

0	1	2	3	4
Never	Sometimes	Half of the time	Often	Almost Always

The upsetting, harmful things that happened to me in my life...

____ 11) left me feeling people can't be trusted, helped me give up on trusting people.

____ 12) took away my confidence that I can make it on my own, left me too needy and trusting.

____ 13) took away my confidence that some people will always be there for me or left me having problems getting close to others and problems sticking with relationships.

____ 14) helped me stay in bad relationships too long, feeling like I didn't deserve any better or couldn't get anyone else.

____ 15) left me not caring enough about myself.

____ 16) left me not caring enough about others.

____ 17) left me feeling I have to always try harder and do more.

____ 18) helped me give up on trying hard because I was afraid of failing.

____ 19) left me afraid to try new things (school/mental, sports/physical and social/meet people)

I would usually try things that were- __really easy and I knew I could do;

__a bit of a challenge; __really hard; __ I would not usually try anything new

Why? _____

_____

_____

____ 20) made me afraid of doing well because then I would feel pressure to keep it up.

____ 21) left me feeling I can't make it on my own and got me going from one relationship to another.

____ 22) left me wanting to get even with those who were responsible.

____ 23) left me feeling like giving up on my life and just ending it.

____ 24) left me feeling like giving up on dealing with my unwanted feelings by getting high.

____ 25) left me feeling like giving up on responsibilities by bailing out when I get stressed.

____ 26) left me feeling like a failure.

___ 27) left me with an "I can't" belief about succeeding in life.

___ 28) left me feeling that whatever happens to me is fate and there is nothing I can do about it.

D. Self-Control: Review the section above to get back in touch with how the top three <u>upsetting things, past hurt or trauma that you listed on your Link #1 summary have left you feeling and made it difficult for you to master, do or try things.</u>

Use the numbered ratings on the scale below to rate how likely you would be to have problems with self-control in each situation listed below.

0	1	2	3	4
Not at all	Somewhat	Moderately	Highly	Extremely

How likely are you to lose self-control and do or say something you shouldn't when you...

___ 1) are very **frustrated and angry**?

___ 2) are very **anxious and afraid**?

___ 3) are very **sad and depressed**?

___ 4) are feeling **sexually excited or aroused**?

___ 5) are going over and over **something recent that was done wrong to you** and can see the person who did it across the room?

___ 6) are **around negative peers** who work you up by saying you are justified in feeling the way you do and encourage you to do a harmful behavior?

___ 7) are **drinking or getting high**?

___ 8) are in a **conflict or heated argument** with someone who won't back down?

___ 9) are by yourself and **going over and over something** that was unjust, wrong or upsetting?

___ 10) are going over and over **something in the past that was done wrong to you** and are all by yourself?

Describe the most recent situation where you lost self-control and justified your actions based on the feelings you were having, the thoughts you were having or the peers who worked you up.

_____

_____

_____

_____

_____

_____

_____

_____

E. Link 2- Social-Emotional Maturity Structured Discovery Exercise

Review the social maturity (i.e., honesty, trust, loyalty, concern and responsibility) problems listed above and the emotional maturity (i.e., self-awareness, self-efficacy and self-control) problems you have experienced in section A, B, C and D (p. 29- 36). Then:

1) List the top three <u>upsetting</u> feelings (i.e., the ones that you rated highest) that you have experienced during or when thinking about your past hurts or abuses (from section B):

Most upsetting feeling _____

2nd most upsetting feeling _____

3rd most upsetting feeling _____

Where did the top three feelings you listed above come from? What situations were you usually in when experiencing those feelings?

_____

_____

_____

_____

2) List the #1 most important mental tasks, physical behaviors and social activity (i.e., the ones that you wish you had been able to do the most) that you haven't tried to do or master (from section C):

#1 Mental task _____

#1 Physical behavior _____

#1 Social activity _____

How has not doing the things you listed above affected you?

_____

_____

_____

_____

What do you think held you back from doing those things?

_____

_____

_____

What did you do to make up for or compensate for not being able to do the important things that you wished you could?

_____

_____

_____

3) List the top three situations (i.e., the ones that you rated highest in section D) where you are most likely to lose self-control.

_____

_____

_____

What makes it difficult for you to control yourself in these situations? (**Hint:** Don't forget to consider your thoughts, feelings and human needs for acceptance, attention or excitement)

_____

_____

_____

_____

_____

What would make it easier to stay on track? (**Hint:** Is it easier to escape or avoid trouble ? p. 51).

_____

_____

_____

4) Compare your social maturity ratings in section A to your upset over past problems and self-awareness sentences in section B, your self-efficacy ratings in section C and your self-control ratings in section D. List any connections that you are able to make between these aspects or parts of your life (i.e., Section A, B, C & D, p. 29- 36).

Connections example- "My secret keeping and dishonesty about my problems in school (section A) was related to my feelings of anger and embarrassment (section B) from being told I would never amount to anything. This led me to tell myself 'I won't be able to make it anyway so why even try' and giving up on trying to do positive things (mental- homework, physical- baseball and social- dances) with positive people in school (section C). Giving up on trying positive things, left me with no place to fit in with positive people. This steered me towards hanging out with negative people. So I started getting high with 'the burnouts' for acceptance which made shoplifting for attention and excitement easy (section D). I ended up putting what I wanted (acceptance) before what I needed (achievement), dropped out of school and got arrested for harmful behavior (theft/drugs). I always put other people's wants before my needs. I would do too much for others, go along to get along and compromise myself to be accepted."

Use the "Connections example" (p. 38) to help you list the connections between your social maturity (section A) self-awareness (section B), self-efficacy (section C) and self-control (section D) below.

_____

_____

_____

_____

_____

_____

_____

Now "Solve the problem" by listing and what you can do about it now in section 5 below.

5) Explain how you can use your three SET problem solving steps (p. 13) to solve the problem of how to do the mental, physical and social activities that you wish you had been able to do (listed earlier in section E- 2, p. 37). In order to, "Solve the problem" you need to: 1) <u>S</u>et your goal; 2) <u>E</u>valuate your progress and options; 3) <u>T</u>ake responsible action.

Here is a **SET problem solving example** using the school problem described earlier in the "Connections example" (section 4, page 38).
"After I got in trouble, I had to get honest about my real goal to be accepted. Although I now realize that everyone wants to be accepted and no one wants to be rejected, this was hard for me because of my attitude that I didn't need anyone's acceptance or care what they thought about me. I had to admit that acceptance was more important to me than the other students because they got it from family and I didn't. Once I got honest about my real and slightly embarrassing goal to be accepted, evaluating my progress and options was easy. In evaluating my progress, the answer to the question 'How well is what I am doing working in getting me what I want?' was simple. I was getting lots of acceptance getting high with my burnout peers. As an added plus, suggesting thrill crimes gave me even more acceptance in a negative leader role and doing them was exciting. The question 'How will things likely to turn out for me if I continue this way?' was already answered. I am in court-ordered residential treatment filling out this workbook. I put my feelings, getting accepted and getting high before thinking about the consequences of losing my freedom. Evaluating my options was a total 'no brainer'. I have two simple choices, go back to getting acceptance like I did before and risk losing my freedom again or find a way to get acceptance that doesn't risk losing my freedom. The decision to 'Take responsible action' by answering the question, 'What should I try first?' takes more courage than thought. I can always get high with the burnouts, they will always accept me but if I want acceptance without risking my freedom, I need to get up the courage to change. This means listening to my counselor about getting acceptance from teachers and positive peers. To do this I will need to start showing interest in what the teachers are talking about, get a tutor to help me out, get myself back on the baseball team and start going to the school dances to make some positive friends."

Use the "SET problem solving example" (p. 39) to help you solve a real life problem (E- 2, p. 37). Set your goal; Evaluate your progress and options; Take responsible action.

_____
_____
_____
_____
_____
_____
_____
_____
_____
_____
_____
_____
_____
_____
_____

6) **Link #2 Summary Completion Instructions-** Identify your #1 Social Maturity Problem (from Section A above) and circling the highest rating. Then identify your #1 Self-Awareness, Self-Efficacy (confidence) and Self-Control problems that you disclosed in sections B, C and D by circling the highest rating in each category. Record at least your #1 social maturity, self-awareness, self-efficacy and self-control problems on the Risk Factor Chain worksheet (page 81) at the end of this section. If you have a tie (i.e., more than one serious social maturity, self-awareness, self-efficacy or self-control problem, put the most important problems on the first page and use the second page "continued" portion of your Risk Factor Chain worksheet to list the other important problems. Imagine yourself teaching someone else about this part of your life. Put your important descriptions in phrase form that makes it easy for you to explain and makes sense when read by others. Don't limit yourself to the #1 self-awareness, self-efficacy & self-control points if there are important parts that fit in this area. Make sure that you do not leave out any important information about yourself on this topic. Use the margins if needed.

Get honest about your Social-Emotional Maturity Problems. Think about who you are and what you stand for (see p. 27 & 82) along with your confidence and self-control. Discuss this with your therapist or group if you are in treatment. Log the date you discussed these issues and who you discussed them with below.

Date: _____ Discussed with: _____

The Risk Factor Chain: LINK #3- Situational Risk Factors
(High Risk Situations for Harmful Behavior)

"Be careful the friends you choose for you will become like them."-- W. Clement Stone (1902- 2002)

Name: _____   **Date:** _____

Definition: Situational Risk Factors include "High risk situations" that put you at risk for relapse. High risk situations involve people, places, circumstances, thoughts or feelings that can trigger falling back into unhealthy behavior that is harmful to yourself or others. These situations include harmful behavior triggers such as getting very upset or angry, being around others who are encouraging you and being in places where unhealthy behavior is being done by others or harmful behavior is not likely to result in consequences. High risk situations provide you with motive or opportunity for relapse. In order to decide what is a high risk situation for you, you must use your knowledge about your past harmful behavior. High Risk Situations can be connected to Link 2 low self-efficacy (low confidence in your ability to be effective) in cases where the risky situation acts to make you feel more effective, competent, powerful or acts to relieve feelings of helplessness, incompetence or powerlessness. Examples include controlling mood with tobacco, alcohol/drugs or food as well as controlling others with seduction, manipulation or force. High risk situations typically involve people, places and things (including feelings) that trigger harmful behavior. Three common high risk situations for multiple forms of harmful behavior are access, trigger feelings and trigger thoughts which are considered negative social influence from high risk people if they are stated by others. Some basic examples are listed below.

Unhealthy, Harmful Behavior	Access (High risk places)	Trigger Feeling	Trigger Thoughts or Negative Social Influence (High risk people)
Unhealthy eating	All you can eat buffet	Depressed	"You have to try this"
Over-spending	Outlet mall	Depressed	"You deserve it after the day you had"
Cigarette smoking	Smoke filled party	Boredom	"Have a cigarette"
Drinking	Bar	Anxious	"Have a drink to relax "
Marijuana smoking	Party	Happy	"It's just weed, no big deal"
Physical violence	Person insulting you	Anger	"Are you going to take that crap?"
Sexual imposition	Intoxicated party girl	Arousal	"Go ahead, she wants it"

Risk Factor Question #3: What situations seem to precede the harmful behavior?

A. **List the primary type of harmful behavior** that resulted in your referral for treatment or that you need to change (i.e., that you listed on page 4), **and** two other harmful, harmful behaviors that you believe you need to put in check (i.e., your top 3).

1)_____ 2)_____ 3)_____

B. **High risk people.** Negative social influence is a powerful relapse trigger. Complete the Harmful Behavior Social Diagram on the following page and use it to help you answer the questions below about the high risk people in your life.

> **Hint:** List family and friends who had a problem or got in trouble and what it was, e.g., Mom:, overeating, smoking; Dad: physical and trust abuse- beating mom and cheating on her; Brother: Sexual abuse- Jail for molesting me and sister; Uncle: drug rehab; Friend Bill: substance abuse

Harmful Behavior Social Diagram Worksheet

List the people you know who have been involved in unhealthy, harmful, abusive or excessive behaviors along with their names and types of harmful behaviors, e.g., sexual; physical; property (spending, gambling); substance (drugs, alcohol, cigarettes, food) or; trust (cheating, bullying) abuse problems.

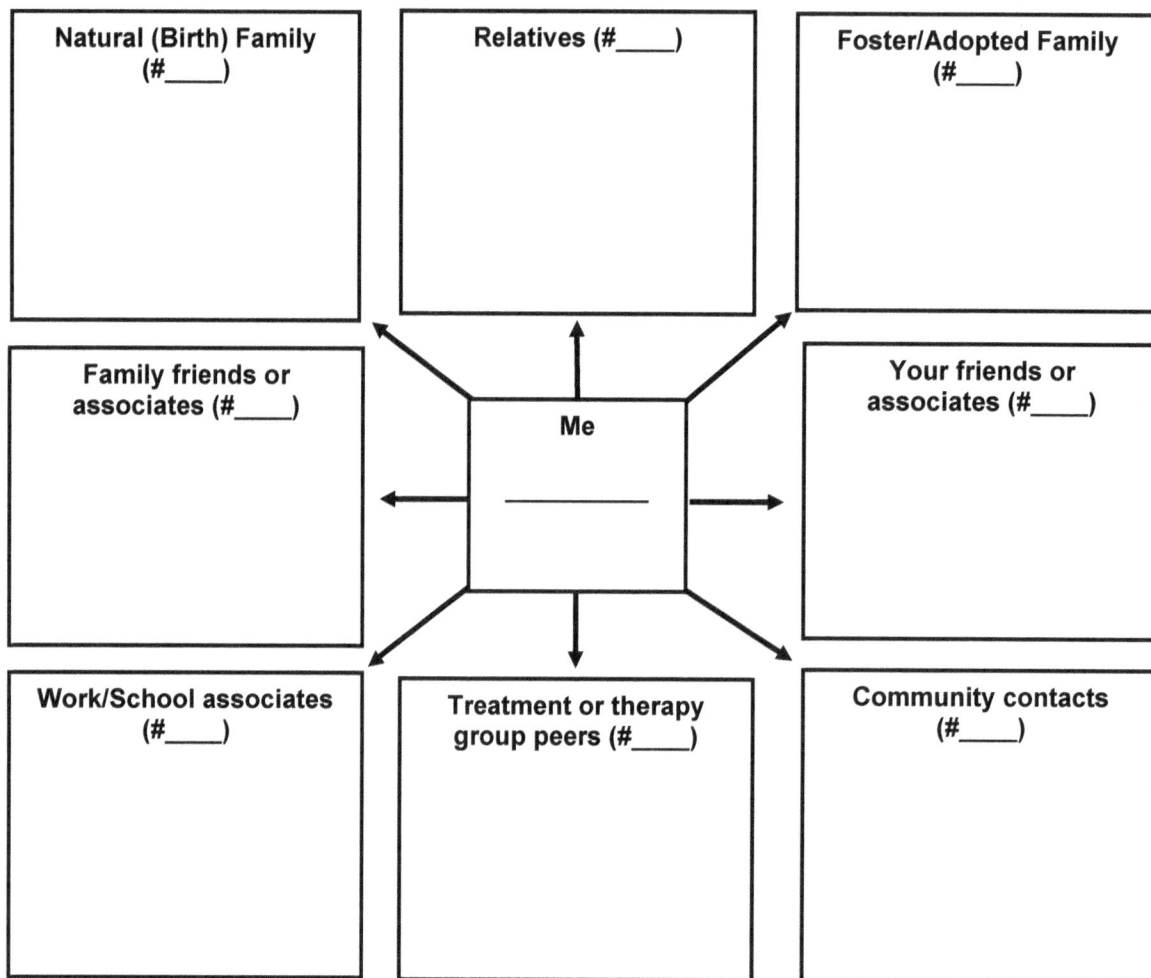

Natural (Birth) Family (#____)	Relatives (#____)	Foster/Adopted Family (#____)
Family friends or associates (#____)	Me	Your friends or associates (#____)
Work/School associates (#____)	Treatment or therapy group peers (#____)	Community contacts (#____)

1. Think about the <u>unhealthy, harmful behavior that resulted in your referred for treatment</u>. Underline the people on your social diagram who have been referred to treatment for the same reason that you have or who have had the same problems.
2. High risk situations with people involves too many people or not enough. For example, being around lots of people doing the wrong thing (e.g., drug party), being around one person you can do the wrong thing to (e.g., target victim of sexual abuse) or being by yourself so you can do the wrong thing and no one will know (e.g., unhealthy eating or drinking). If one of your high risk people was you being alone, write "being alone" under "Me" in your Harmful Behavior Social Diagram.
3. Have you ever pulled anyone else into an unhealthy harmful behavior? ___Yes; ___No.

   List who, what you did and why _____

   _____

4. Have any of the people in your Harmful Behavior Social Diagram ever pulled you into an unhealthy harmful behavior? ___Yes; ___No.   List who, what you did and why.

Who (Names)   What you did.   Why you did it

_____

_____

_____

_____

Who usually started it, you or them? ___Usually me; ___Usually them; ___About half & half

5. Review your answers to questions 2 and 3 above, then list your high risk people and why you believe they are high risk for you to be around.

Who (Names)   Why they are high risk for triggering relapse back into my problem

_____

_____

_____

_____

Basic Human Emotions: 101

Human beings exposed to the harmful, stressful, traumatic historical events listed in Link #1 are often left with unwanted feelings that don't go away. Three basic types of unwanted feelings are anger, anxiety and depression. These emotions range in severity from mild to severe and may be begin during the stressful event or may be delayed until much later in time. Anger can range from a mild annoyance to a moderate anger to a severe rage and may be include continuous thoughts about unjust treatment and a desire for revenge. Anxiety can range from mild social discomfort to a moderate anxiety (fear) to a severe panic attack and may include continuous thoughts about something bad happening. Depression can range from a mild sadness to a moderate feeling of depression (including feeling helpless) to suicidal despair (including feeling hopeless) and may include continuous thoughts about giving up.

Situations can Trigger Feelings: Some Basic Examples

Situation	Feeling
Someone puts you down in front of others who laugh out loud.	Anger
As you enter a store, an armed robber comes running out and points his gun at you.	Anxiety
You are visiting your best friend who is dying in the hospital	Depression

C. What's in it for me? What does your primary form of harmful behavior do for you?
List your #1 harmful behavior from section "A" above here _____
and describe what you get out of it, what it does for you below.

Use the numbered ratings on the scale below to rate how much doing your harmful behavior decreased feelings you didn't want or increased feelings you did want.

0	1	2	3	4
Not at all	**A Little**	**Moderately**	**Quite A Bit**	**Extremely**

___ 1) Decreases anger/frustration

___ 2) Decreases anxiety/tension

___ 3) Decreases depression/sadness

___ 4) Decreases boredom

___ 5) Decreases loneliness

___ 6) Decreases helplessness

___ 7) Decreases feeling inferior, inadequate or less than others

___ 8) Decreases guilt and shame

___ 9) Decreases feeling overwhelmed and stressed out

___10) Decreases feeling rejected and put Down

___11) Increases patience

___12) Increases relaxation, feeling calm

___13) Increases feeling good, happiness, joy

___14) Increases excitement, a thrill or "rush"

___15) Increases social confidence, ability talk to others, get social attention

___16) Increases feelings of power, being in control

___17) Increases feeling more adequate or capable than others

___18) Increases general confidence and feeling like you can succeed

___19) Increases relief, helps feel normal

___20) Increases feeling accepted, fitting in

Acting out feelings 101

Unwanted feelings usually only go two directions, in on you (e.g., eating, drinking, cutting) or out on others (e.g., hitting, stealing, cheating, fondling). Any basic human emotion can be a **"trigger feeling"** that motivates acting out feelings through behavior that is harmful to self or others. Different people get triggered by different feelings. To handle your unhealthy, harmful behavior you need to know your trigger feelings. Look at the ratings on the feelings that you were getting from your harmful behavior. Use the space below to write a brief summary of what your harmful behavior does for you.

_____

_____

_____

_____

_____

Feelings from Situations can Trigger Relapse: Some Basic Examples

Feeling	Harmful Behavior Relapse
You get very angry after someone puts you down in front of others who laugh out loud.	Punched him out (Physical abuse)
You get very anxious after seeing an armed robber who points his gun at you while running out of a store.	Lied to the store owner and police about seeing his face (Trust abuse)
You get very depressed after visiting your best friend who is dying in the hospital.	Got drunk or high afterwards (Substance abuse)

D. Use the numbers on the scale below to **rate how likely you are to relapse when experiencing the following TRIGGER FEELINGS.**

0	1	2	3	4
Not at all	**Somewhat**	**Moderately**	**Highly**	**Extremely**

____ 1) A minor amount of anger (i.e., ANNOYANCE) toward someone or about something that happened.

____ 2) Fairly strong ANGER toward someone or about something that happened.

____ 3) Severe anger (i.e., RAGE) toward someone or about something that happened.

____ 4) A minor amount of fear/anxiety (i.e., SOCIAL DISCOMFORT) around someone or about something that happened.

____ 5) Fairly strong FEAR/ANXIETY around someone or about something that happened.

____ 6) Severe fear/anxiety (i.e., PANIC) around someone or about something that happened.

____ 7) A minor amount of depression (i.e., SADNESS) about something that happened.

____ 8) Fairly strong DEPRESSION & HELPLESSNESS about something that happened.

____ 9) Severe depression (i.e., DESPAIR & total HELPLESSNESS) about something that happened.

____10) A minor amount of GUILT & SHAME about something that happened.

____11) Fairly strong GUILT & SHAME about something that happened.

____12) Severe GUILT & SHAME about something that happened.

____13) A minor amount of STRESS & FEELING OVERWHELMED about something that happened.

____14) Fairly strong STRESS & FEELING OVERWHELMED about something that happened.

____15) Severe STRESS & FEELING OVERWHELMED about something that happened.

____16) A minor amount of REJECTION & INADEQUACY (feeling less than others or put down) about something that happened.

Use the numbers on the scale below to rate how likely you are to relapse when experiencing the following TRIGGER FEELINGS.

0	1	2	3	4
Not at all	Somewhat	Moderately	Highly	Extremely

___17) Fairly strong REJECTION & INADEQUACY (feeling less than others or put down) about something that happened.

___18) Severe REJECTION & INADEQUACY (feeling less than others or put down) about something that happened.

___19) A minor amount of relationship JEALOUSY or insecurity over something that happened.

___20) Fairly strong relationship JEALOUSY or insecurity over something that happened.

___21) Severe relationship JEALOUSY or insecurity over something that happened.

___22) Feeling insecure do to a lack of closure and things being up in the air that you want resolved

23) List any other feelings that you have learned may put you at risk for relapse. Get feedback from your treatment group and/or therapist.

_____

_____

_____

24) Who in your life triggers most of the feelings above that you have rated moderately or higher in the section above? Add the names of those people in the correct box on your Harmful Behavior Social Diagram.

High Risk Situations that Can Trigger Relapse: Some Basic Examples

High Risk Situation	Basic Example	Harmful Behavior Relapse
Problem people	Two youth get in an argument in a group home. Several problem peers gather around yelling and trying and stir up a fight.	One youth punches the other and is arrested for assault (physical abuse). The other youth runs away that night to get high and relieve stress (substance abuse).
Unwanted feelings	Three adults attend a loved one's funeral. One gets depressed over the loss, a second gets angry at the person who did it and the third becomes anxious that they will never find anyone else.	The first blows their diet at the all you can eat buffet (food abuse). The second blows off their Alcoholics Anonymous meeting and goes to a bar (substance abuse). The third picks up an underage prostitute (sex abuse).
Access to unhealthy, harmful activities	A youth with a shoplifting problem goes to the mall with no money and sees a new pair of tennis shoes he really likes.	He tries on a pair, puts his shoes in the box, puts the box back on the shelf and walks out the door without paying (property abuse).

E. Use the numbered ratings on the scale below to **rate how likely you are to relapse when in the following TRIGGER SITUATIONS.**

0 Not at all	1 Somewhat	2 Moderately	3 Highly	4 Extremely

___ 1) Have unhealthy, harmful thoughts.

___ 2) Have unhealthy, harmful **urges or feelings**.

___ 3) Have a **plan** to commit harmful behavior.

___ 4) Have **access** to your primary form of harmful behavior such as specific abuse substance (e.g., drug of choice, alcohol, cigarettes, favorite food), target people (e.g., individuals you like to pick on, have sex with, get high with, smoke or overeat or that encourage you to do these things) or high risk situation (e.g., are in places where you have let go of your self-control or done the wrong thing in the past).

___ 5) Have access to abuse substances, target person(s) or objects which are similar to your abuse substance, target person(s) or high risk situation.

___ 6) Have a job that puts you around your primary form of harmful behavior (abuse substance, target people or objects of choice).

___ 7) Hang out in places where your primary form of harmful behavior is easily available.

___ 8) Hang out with others who have the same or similar harmful behavior problems.

___ 9) Have **thoughts/plans, feelings/urges and access** to your primary form of harmful behavior.

___10) Are being threatened by someone.

___11) Experience social stress- Being in a social situation such as a party where you are expected to start conversations with others.

___12) Experience sexual tension- Being alone with someone you may get sexual feelings around.

___13) Are being made fun of, put down or called names.

___14) Are alone too much.

___15) Are being left out, not feeling accepted or feeling unwanted.

___16) Are holding feelings and opinions inside and not asserting self.

___17) Are feeling disappointed in yourself, ineffective and powerless

___18) Are getting yourself further upset by not trying to look at things from another persons point of view and ruminating (going over and over something that was not fair).

___19) Are not thinking of how another person might feel if you do or say something.

Use the numbered ratings on the scale below to **rate how likely you are to relapse when in the following TRIGGER SITUATIONS.**

0 Not at all	1 Somewhat	2 Moderately	3 Highly	4 Extremely

___20) Are not thinking of the possible consequences of each action I take.

___21) Are letting your feelings get in the way of your seeing what is being said about you.

___22) Are not accepting feedback even though more than one person says that I'm wrong or have a problem.

___23) Are having a relationship conflict or struggle over who is to get their way.

___24) Are experiencing a relationship loss.

___25) Are with a partner, parent, guardian or others who are not supportive, deny your problem, minimize your problem or blame others.

___26) Avoid talking about your feelings in group or individual therapy.

___27) Letting your thoughts get out of control and not bringing it up in group or individual therapy.

___28) Are being lazy and not completing your responsibilities.

___29) Are cutting corners and taking risks.

___30 Are with a gang who encourage negative, risky, illegal, destructive or abusive actions.

31) **Discuss the SITUATIONS that you have learned may put you at risk for relapse.** Get feedback from your treatment group and/or therapist. Now look through the above questions and think about what in your life triggers most of your relapse problems (items rated moderately or higher in the section above). Use the space below to put together an example of how problem people, unwanted feelings and access to unhealthy, harmful activities led to a relapse.

_____

_____

_____

_____

_____

_____

32) Since committing one type of harmful behavior can trigger another, it is important to look at all forms of harmful behavior as possible trigger situations for other forms. Examples of how one type of harmful behavior can trigger another are listed on the next page.

Primary Problem (Why you were referred for treatment or what you consider your biggest problem)	Trigger Behavior	Connection between primary problem and trigger behavior (What you said to yourself that allowed one harmful behavior to trigger another)
Food abuse (overeating)	Drinking (Alcohol abuse)	"I already violated by diet by going out drinking so I might as well eat what I want"
Drug abuse	Fighting (Physical abuse)	"I already violated my parole by fighting so I might as well get high"
Trust abuse (lying)	Stealing (Property abuse)	"I already stole so I might as well lie about it"
Responsibility abuse/neglect	Marijuana abuse	"I already got high at lunch so I might as well blow off the rest of the day"
Sexual abuse	Compulsive deviant pornography use	"I already got aroused looking at porno so I might as well do what I want"
Sexual acting out	Cocaine abuse	"I already did coke with this person so I might as well have sex"

The "Slip Give-Up Trigger"- explains the connection between the primary problem and trigger behavior because slipping on one harmful behavior triggers giving up on another. Slipping and giving up is pretty common. Use the space below to write an example of how you have slipped up with one harmful behavior, then given up on self-control and did another harmful behavior.

_____

_____

_____

_____

F. Link 3- High Risk Situations Summary

Review your answers to the questions about your high risk situations and write a brief summary listing the feelings, people, places, situations and things that put you at risk for a relapse by providing you with either motive or opportunity for relapse. Record the top three types of harmful behavior that you listed in section A above in the chart below. If you have been referred for treatment of a harmful behavior list that as your #1 problem.

High Risk Situation Worksheet

Unhealthy, Harmful Behavior	High Risk People (see your Harmful Behavior Social Diagram)	High Risk Places or Situations	High Risk Feelings & Thoughts
Harmful behavior #1 (_____)			

Harmful Behavior	High Risk People	High Risk Places	High Risk Feelings & Thoughts
Harmful behavior #2 (_____)			
Harmful behavior #3 (_____)			

Identify the connections between your harmful behaviors by circling the similar people, places, situations, feelings in section F above. What are the similar high risk situations that you notice in all three types of harmful behavior that you could get into? What can you do about this now?

_____

_____

_____

_____

_____

(If you need more space, use the workspace on page 79, 116 or the inside of the front and back covers)

G. Link #3 Summary Completion Instructions- Review your answers to the questions in section F above and record at least the top three High Risk Situations that had the strongest effect in setting the occasion for your primary form harmful behavior **on the Risk Factor Chain worksheet (page 81)** at the end of this section (use the "continued" portion of your worksheet if needed). Imagine yourself teaching someone else about this part of your life. Put your important descriptions in phrase form that makes it easy for you to explain and makes sense when read by others. Don't limit yourself to the top three points if there are important parts that fit in this area. Make sure that you do not leave out any important information on this topic. Use the margins if needed. Use the space below to make a Relapse Prevention Plan detaining what high risk situations you need to avoid and how you will avoid them. The basic Relapse Prevention Plan steps are as follows: 1) Awareness training- Identify high risk situations for relapse (behavior "triggers"); 2) Positive planning- Develop High Risk Situation avoidance strategies (written) and; 3) Reinforced practice on things that could go wrong- Rehearse emergency strategies with therapist and group (who asks "What if…" questions).

Relapse Prevention Rule #1, "Planning Power beats Willpower"

In Social Responsibility Therapy, our number one responsibility is self-control. Self-control is maintained by avoiding and escaping high risk situations. The easiest way to maintain self-control of unhealthy, harmful behavior is to learn how to avoid high risk situations. Always use positive planning to avoid high risk situations because harmful behavior is far easier to avoid than to stop once you get started. This rule can be traced back to the early Roman philosophers…

It is easier to exclude harmful passions than to rule them,
and to deny them admittance than to control them after they have been admitted.

-- Seneca (5 BC - 65 AD)

The conclusion to be drawn from this age old insight is that successful management of harmful behavior depends more on developing planning power than inheriting willpower.

Relapse Prevention Plan- Use your High Risk Situation Worksheet on page 49- 50

1. My high risk situations for relapse (harmful behavior "triggers") are:

   People:_____

   _____

   Places (access):_____

   _____

   Feelings:_____

   _____

   Thoughts (Hint: see "Slip Give-Up Trigger" p. 49):_____

   _____

2. My positive plans to deal with these situations are:

   People:_____

   _____

   Places (access):_____

   _____

   Feelings:_____

   _____

   Thoughts:_____

   _____

3. Things that could go wrong and how I need to respond are:

   People:_____

   Places (access):_____

Feelings:_____

Thoughts:_____

H. If you can't avoid high risk situations, use your Three Step Social Responsibility Plan to escape them (see p. 11). It does you no good to develop your self-awareness to the point where you can recognize a high risk situation if you stay in that situation until a relapse is triggered. Whenever you become aware of a high risk situation you need to immediately Avoid Trouble with your Three Step Social Responsibility Plan to "Get out, Get Honest and Get Responsible". These three basic steps involve: 1) getting out of or avoiding the high risk situation; 2) getting rid of the negative, irresponsible thoughts that were triggered by that situation (See Appendix C, p. 94) and; 3) substituting a positive socially responsible thought that will help you avoid harmful behavior. Discuss the Three Step Social Responsibility Plan with your therapist or in your treatment group and practice applying it to your high risk situations.

Explain how you can use your ACTS healthy behavior success skills (p. 11) to deal with of your high risk people, places, feelings and thoughts.

People:_____

_____

_____

Places (access):_____

_____

_____

Feelings:_____

_____

_____

> **Hint: Handling high risk feelings-** Although unwanted feelings usually go in on you or out on others, you actually have a third choice. You can calm yourself down and let your feelings go.

Thoughts (Appendix C, p. 94): _____

_____

_____

Get honest about your High Risk Situations and Relapse Prevention Plan. Set a daily relapse prevention/responsibility plan and update it every morning, e.g. "Today I will escape…, avoid… and maintain…" (See Link 3, p. 84). Discuss this with your therapist or group if you are in treatment and make changes to your plan (above) based on the feedback you receive. Log the date you discussed these issues and who you discussed them with in the space provided below.

Date: _____ Discussed with: _____

The Risk Factor Chain: LINK #4- Cognitive Risk Factors
(Irresponsible Thinking that Supports Harmful Behavior)

"We cannot solve our problems with the same thinking we used when we created them."--Albert Einstein

Name: _____   **Date**: _____

Definition: Cognitive Risk Factors involve Irresponsible Thinking that supports and allows irresponsible behavior that is harmful to self or others. Responsible Thinking supports responsible behavior that is helpful to self or others. Irresponsible behavior is associated with being immature and means not acting responsible by doing the right thing at the right time for the right reason. Irresponsible people do what they want, when they want for the reason they want without thinking about whether their actions could be harmful to self or others. Irresponsible thinking that supports and allows unhealthy, harmful behavior includes thinking errors, irrational beliefs, false conclusions, false perceptions and cognitive disinhibitors (thoughts that disinhibit or break down your resistance to unhealthy, harmful behavior). In order to substitute more appropriate, responsible thinking, you need to become aware of the irresponsible thinking that supports and allows harmful behavior. Irresponsible thinking increases the risk of harmful behavior by justifying or minimizing dwelling on harmful behavior thoughts or plans, entering or staying in high risk situations for harmful behavior, or pushing back the line on what you know is wrong and heading for trouble. Not being aware of Irresponsible Thinking puts you at risk for repeating behavior that is harmful to yourself or others.

Risk Factor Question #4: What did you say to yourself before, during and after the harmful behavior?

Awareness and Honesty Examination

Self-awareness and honesty about yourself is very important in your treatment. The following "Awareness and Honesty Examination" is made up of questions designed to see *how aware you are* of the way you think, act and talk to yourself along with *how honest you can be* about your thoughts, feelings and behavior. Everyone makes mistakes and has problems dealing with things that happen to them from time to time. Everyone slips and does things they shouldn't even though they have a feeling that what they are considering may be wrong.

The following Awareness and Honesty Examination covers cognitive risk factors along with social responsibility problems that support harmful behavior and prevent getting the most out of treatment. The items on this exam include ways that people think and act when handling unfortunate events, making mistakes, getting in trouble, conflicts or doing something they shouldn't that could be harmful to self or others.

Taking this exam is the exact opposite of the typical classroom test, job interview or first date where the object is to make yourself look good in order to "score" highly or do well in making a positive impression. In this task, since the object is self-awareness and honesty, "When you're looking bad, you're looking good", that is when you are aware of shortcomings or problem areas and get honest about them (i.e., look bad), you get the highest honesty and awareness score (i.e., look good). Think about each question and mark it if you are aware of it or if you have been made aware of it by others (told that you do it or confronted about it).

When dealing with past situations, please rate how often you have had the following thoughts or behaviors.

Use the numbered ratings on the scale below to rate your answers to the following questions.

0	1	2	3	4
Never	Sometimes	Half of the time	Often	Almost Always

When dealing with past situations, please rate how often you have...

____ 1. Told others what you thought they wanted to hear, not exactly what happened.

____ 2. Not being polite to others while expecting or demanding respect for yourself.

____ 3. Held on to a relationship where you put in more than you got out.

____ 4. Told yourself or others that "you've got to look out for number one" because nobody else will or thought that in life it's "every man for himself".

____ 5. Told yourself "I give up, there's no use in trying".

____ 6. Said "I forgot" or "you forgot to tell me" when reminded about something you knew you were supposed to do.

____ 7. Told yourself that becoming successful is more important than anything else in life.

____ 8. Not been exactly sure why you have done some of the things that you did.

____ 9. Told yourself that you will stay in control and never let anyone hurt you, take advantage of you or get the best of you again.

____ 10. Felt I could do anything if I wasn't held back by others or situations.

____ 11. Felt that people would look down on you if you showed your emotions, admitted you were wrong or admitted a mistake.

____ 12. Went along with things you wouldn't normally do or that you knew were wrong in order to fit in, be accepted, be socially comfortable or avoid being put down.

____ 13. Not written down things that needed to get done and didn't get them turned in or completed.

____ 14. Borrowed things without asking or forgot to return borrowed items.

____ 15. Told yourself that what you did wasn't that bad because you did it on rare occasions, when stressed out or when using drugs/alcohol.

____ 16. Told yourself or others that what happened wasn't your fault because someone else got you upset or you always get blamed whether you did wrong or not.

____ 17. Justified actions based on feelings- For example, told yourself the other person deserved what you said or did because they got you upset or told yourself that you deserved to do something harmful (eating, drinking, smoking, drugs) because you were upset.

____ 18. Thought that if people aren't with you, they're against you.

0	1	2	3	4
Never	Sometimes	Half of the time	Often	Almost Always

When dealing with past situations, please rate how often you have...

___ 19. Jumped to conclusions based on how the situation looked at the time.

___ 20. Told yourself or others that a problem others caused or mistake they made was worse than it really was and made a big deal about it.

___ 21. Said "Yes" to someone with no intention of doing what they ask.

___ 22. Multiplied criticism you received by two (telling yourself it was really harsh) while dividing the criticism you gave in half (telling yourself you weren't that harsh).

___ 23. Put negative peers/friends before family or positive, responsible peers.

___ 24. Been told or thought that you don't care how your actions might affect others.

___ 25. Felt that things always go wrong and will never work out.

___ 26. Not tried your hardest and done things half way or just enough to get by.

___ 27. Put getting ahead, work or making money (including illegally) before family or friends.

___ 28. Not been aware of feeling any certain way (e.g., sad, anxious, angry) when upset over something.

___ 29. Felt very upset when things didn't go the way you wanted them to and told yourself "This is terrible" or "I can't stand this".

___ 30. Been annoyed by people who know less than me trying to tell me what to do.

___ 31. Found yourself worrying about being put down, looking bad, being embarrassed or messing up in front of others.

___ 32. Done something risky or wrong for attention.

___ 33. Been told that you are not organized.

___ 34. Let joking, teasing or horseplay go too far.

___ 35. When considering doing something wrong or explaining what you did to others, found yourself using the words, "just", "only", "a little", "rarely" or "once".

___ 36. Felt that you couldn't help yourself from getting in trouble because you were encouraged or the other person started it.

___ 37. Given others logical explanations that excuse or justify a mistake you made.

___ 38. Felt like "You're either a hero or a zero", that there is nothing in between and anything less than being number one is not good enough.

___ 39. Made decisions without consulting others because the motivations, attitudes or actions of those involved were clear and there was no need to check out the information that was presented.

___ 40. Told yourself or others that a mistake that you made was horrible, made a big deal out of it and turned it into a really upsetting experience.

0	1	2	3	4
Never	Sometimes	Half of the time	Often	Almost Always

When dealing with past situations, please rate how often you have...

___ 41. Left out parts of a story or told the part of a mistake, error or problem that wasn't so bad and left out parts that were worse.

___ 42. Told yourself that trust should be given to you without considering that your trust in others is earned by their behavior.

___ 43. Defended negative, irresponsible peers or partners that really didn't deserve my support.

___ 44. Told yourself that your behavior only hurts you or if you knew it affected others told yourself "it could be worse".

___ 45. Felt a lack of confidence in yourself.

___ 46. Been told that you are unmotivated or lazy about doing anything you don't want to do (including paying back money you borrow).

___ 47. Told yourself or others that you will do anything it takes to get ahead.

___ 48. Found yourself saying "I don't know" to people who asked you why you did what you did and not really caring to think about it.

___ 49. Played people against people to try and get what you wanted.

___ 50. Felt people have been jealous of your unique and special qualities or talents.

___ 51. Felt that people judge you on your looks so looking good is the most important thing.

___ 52. Gone along with others & made fun of someone that you get along with & think are OK.

___ 53. Had problems because of not thinking ahead about the possible consequences of taking an action or failing to do a responsibility.

___ 54. Found yourself listening in on interesting conversations, asking personal questions or looking through others stuff that they left out.

___ 55. Said to yourself or others "It wasn't that wrong", "It didn't do that much harm", "Others have done it also" or "It wasn't as bad as what others have done".

___ 56. Felt that the situation wasn't fair, you weren't given a chance or you didn't deserve what Happened ("This isn't right") after not doing well or making a mistake.

___ 57. Made a mental list of why what you did was OK or why it will be OK for you to do something that you really shouldn't.

___ 58. Felt like if it can't be done perfectly, why do it at all (or if it can't be done just right, it's not worth doing).

___ 59. Thought that because one thing went wrong or one mistake was made, everything is blown and you might as well quit trying.

___ 60. Told yourself or others that a consequence you received was worse than what really occurred.

___ 61. Lied, misled others or covered things up in order to avoid possible consequences.

___ 62. Considered mistakes you made as accidents but were more likely to view mistakes others made as on purpose.

0	1	2	3	4
Never	Sometimes	Half of the time	Often	Almost Always

When dealing with past situations, please rate how often you have...

___ 63. Covered for someone who has covered for you or kept negative secrets for and with others to cover up problems or mistakes.

___ 64. Been called selfish by a peer, associate, friend, family member or significant other.

___ 65. Told yourself or others excuses for why you can't do something that you are able to do but just don't want to do.

___ 66. Told yourself that the problem was with the job, class or person instead of your ability to handle frustration or disappointment.

___ 67. Been told that when it comes to getting what you want, you don't worry about anyone getting hurt but yourself.

___ 68. Thought things just seem to happen to you for no reason that you have no control over.

___ 69. Showed anger towards others (i.e., sarcasm, annoyance, intimidation, threats or aggressive behavior), used coercion, bribery or manipulation in order to try to get what you wanted.

___ 70. Have had total confidence in your ability to talk your way out of problems or situations.

___ 71. Felt that since people view kindness as weakness, being tough is necessary to get respect.

___ 72. Done something risky or wrong for excitement.

___ 73. Told yourself "Live for today, not for tomorrow" and made your plans based on your needs right now without considering the future effects of your decisions.

___ 74. Been jealous in a relationship, possessive or not wanted others to socialize with someone you really like.

___ 75. Told yourself "Others did it with me (or got me into it) and I'm still alive so it's not that bad if I get others involved".

___ 76. Told yourself or others "He/she did it" or "They caused this problem" when you also had something to do with it.

___ 77. Worked yourself up (e.g., "This isn't right") and then followed your feelings into getting even (e.g., "I'll show you").

___ 78. Thought that "If I can't be the best of the best, I'll be the best of the worst".

___ 79. Assumed that if what you said or did was really a problem, someone would bring it to your attention.

___ 80. Exaggerated or blown something that happened to you so far out of proportion that it was absurd or silly.

___ 81. Been vague with others in order to avoid possible problems.

___ 82. Not asked for help because you thought you should be able to do it on your own or that asking for help shows that you are weak.

___ 83. Complained about others responsibility problems before completing your own.

___ 84. Counted on people who couldn't be counted on and been let down or disappointed.

0	1	2	3	4
Never	Sometimes	Half of the time	Often	Almost Always

When dealing with past situations, please rate how often you have...

____ 85. Said negative things about others or put them down when they were not present to hear what you were saying.

____ 86. Felt like I would never be able to succeed in my life goals.

____ 87. Told yourself "It can wait", "I can do this later" or other excuses to put off doing responsibilities.

____ 88. Told yourself that you had to take what you want or use emotions such as anger, tears or guilt trips to get what you want if asking doesn't work.

____ 89. Paid attention to what you liked (i.e., agreeable feedback from others) and ignored what you didn't want to hear (i.e., disagreeable feedback).

____ 90. Argued to try and win control of the situation or just for the fun of the struggle.

____ 91. Have been 100% confident that I could control or handle problems without making any mistakes.

____ 92. Told yourself or others that being afraid is a weakness.

____ 93. Didn't plan ahead and put things off until the last minute.

____ 94. Stirred up an argument or started a conflict to break up the boredom.

____ 95. Got involved quickly in a relationship that didn't work out.

____ 96. Told yourself or others "You don't understand me".

____ 97. Been told that you are not doing your part of work or family responsibilities or felt that you are not pulling your own weight.

____ 98. Compared yourself to others on TV or the newspaper and thought that other people have a lot more problems.

____ 99. Told yourself "What I'm doing is OK because I'm not really hurting anyone but myself".

____ 100. Told yourself that most things are not accidents and what goes wrong is either your fault or their fault.

____ 101. Kept silent in order to avoid having to discuss a problem.

____ 102. Not spoken up about a problem because you didn't want to be viewed as a "snitch" or felt it was none of your business.

____ 103. Thought that you should be given a chance and trusted but haven't really trusted others.

____ 104. Had something that was done wrong to you (or someone you care about) go over and over in your mind, not been able to let it go.

____ 105. Told yourself that your behavior isn't really a harmful problem and if it does effect you "look at the bright side, it could be worse".

____ 106. Found yourself avoiding responsibilities that you find boring or disagreeable.

____ 107. Been told that you don't see things from anyone else's point of view but your own.

0	1	2	3	4
Never	Sometimes	Half of the time	Often	Almost Always

When dealing with past situations, please rate how often you have...

____ 108. Got others in trouble or did something to get even because they said or did something to you.

____ 109. Felt that others were better than me in one way or another.

____ 110. Told yourself "the best way to deal with problems is to put them out of my mind" .

____ 111. Been late to or missed important appointments.

____ 112. Realized you got too close too quick in a relationship and pulled back fast to get some space.

____ 113. Found yourself getting angry at others and pointing out their problems/issues after they give you some criticism.

____ 114. Thought that unless there is a good chance of achieving your goal right away, it's not worth trying.

____ 115. Felt that I should get more support, attention and concern from others.

____ 116. Told yourself "Even if my behavior is somewhat harmful, lots of people do it" or "Since I only did with others who have already done it before, it's not that bad".

____ 117. Changed the subject or quickly skipped over to another topic when asked about a problem or mistake.

____ 118. Told yourself or others, "If you care about me you should trust me" or used, "You don't trust me" to get your way.

____ 119. Put someone down because what they did or said was dumb from your point of view.

____ 120. Felt there's no real need to change or listen to those who say they want to help me or lashed out at those trying to help me.

____ 121. Put doing something fun before doing responsibilities or work.

____ 122. Ignored what others said without even giving it consideration because you already knew what you were going to do so why even listen.

____ 123. Told yourself "I couldn't ask because they might have said no".

____ 124. Told yourself or others that you were not afraid when you really were.

____ 125. Told yourself that others should cooperate and go along with you more than they do or been disappointed at others lack of cooperation with you.

____ 126. Considered yourself more mature for your age and looked at older people as equals, friends or possible dating partners (now or at any time in your life).

____ 127. Didn't speak up about a problem or tell others what they should know because I didn't want to get someone in trouble or thought "what they don't know won't hurt them".

____ 128. Found yourself looking for support and affection more than looking for the opportunity to give it to others.

0	1	2	3	4
Never	Sometimes	Half of the time	Often	Almost Always

When dealing with past situations, please rate how often you have...

___ 129. Told yourself "Even if my behavior is a problem sometimes, it's a free country so if others don't like it they can hang out with someone else. If they hang around me and something bad happens that effects them, it's their own fault for staying."

___ 130. Complained about aches, pains and a lack of energy to get responsibilities done.

___ 131. Told yourself that you can't learn from people that you don't like or you shouldn't have to listen to people you don't like.

___ 132. Told yourself or others "Why are they lying?" and assuming that others must be lying because they are not reporting things the way you view them.

___ 133. Brought up the problems of others or put them down to make yourself look better.

___ 134. Told yourself it's better to be an offender than a victim (pick on others as opposed to be picked on, take advantage of others as opposed to be conned).

___ 135. Trusted people that seemed OK but you haven't known for long by telling them personal things about yourself or others and been let down.

___ 136. Brought up something to get people arguing and take the heat off of yourself when being confronted about a problem.

___ 137. Insisted that others let you in on things but kept the information you had to yourself.

___ 138. Told yourself that if you can't get a high paying job, it's better not to work at all.

___ 139. Not bothered to pay any attention at all unless the person got your attention by raising their voice or calling everyone's attention to you.

___ 140. Thought that if people don't agree with me, they are probably trying to put me down in front of others because they don't like me.

___ 141. Been angry at others for not trusting you without asking any questions.

___ 142. Told yourself that if you want to maintain the respect of others, you can't back down even on little points.

___ 143. Shifted to another friend for support after a disagreement to let things "cool off".

___ 144. Admitted to a less serious problem or mistake to get people off of the track when asked about a more serious problem or mistake.

___ 145. Been angry at others for shifting their loyalty to other friends or for cheating when you have done the same.

___ 146. Asked yourself why people bother you about finishing things that they could do themselves if it was really that important.

___ 147. Thought that only someone that has had my kind of problem can understand me and help me.

___ 148. Showing anger about being accused without carefully listening to or thinking about the other persons point of view.

___ 149. Felt that if you admit a mistake to others they will probably use it against you.

0	1	2	3	4
Never	Sometimes	Half of the time	Often	Almost Always

When dealing with past situations, please rate how often you have...

____ 150. Pointed out what others who were involved did or that others do it too, in order to take the heat off of yourself.

____ 151. Told yourself that if you are working on a problem area and do something right, people should recognize your accomplishment and treat you like you have changed as opposed to saying "Let's see if you can keep it up".

____ 152. When someone in authority was talking, found yourself ignoring them.

____ 153. Told yourself or others that people can't be trusted so it is always best to keep things to yourself.

____ 154. Confronted others honesty without first getting honest yourself.

____ 155. Have been told or thought that you have had problems finishing what you started.

____ 156. Felt that if others don't go along or cooperate with you like they should, you will have to do something about it or take things into your own hands and/or told yourself, "It's only wrong if you get caught".

____ 157. Thought that people with the same problems that I have are no better off than me and have no right to act like they can help me.

____ 158. Added unnecessary facts or statements to a story (i.e., purposefully made it too long or got it off track) in order to take the focus off of the main issue and avoid problems.

____ 159. Complained about unfair responsibility assignments before completing them.

____ 160. Told yourself that if others don't keep track of their things, they don't really care about them so there's no need to return those things unless asked.

Please list and other thoughts or things that you say to yourself that have caused past problems. Add feedback from your treatment group, therapist, family or partner about their view.

_____

_____

Look over your ratings. List any patterns or connections that you notice on the items you rated.

_____

_____

Go over your answers to the Awareness and Honesty questions to make sure that you have been completely accurate. Then make a photocopy of these results and turn them into your therapist before continuing any further assignments in this workbook.

I have answered this examination honestly and to the best of my ability without any attempt to make myself look better or worse than my past behavior would indicate.

Signature: _____   **Date Completed:** _____

Awareness and Honesty Examination Scoring Sheet

The following structured discovery exercise was designed to help you clarity which of 20 key types of errors in thinking, cognitive distortions and other social responsibility problems, set the occasion for behavior that was harmful to yourself or others in the past.

A. **Identify the types of irresponsible thinking that you have used in the past.**
    At this point, you should have completed your Awareness and Honesty Exam and be ready to identify the types of irresponsible thinking that you have made in the past using the scoring sheet below.

Awareness and Honesty Exam Scoring Instructions

Review what you have reported about yourself on your "Awareness and Honesty Examination" questions and record your 0- 4 rating for each question in the blank space provided before each question number in the "Exam Questions" column on the scoring sheet. Add up all exam questions in each of the 20 Irresponsible Thinking categories listed. Divide the total of all question ratings in each category by the total number of questions in each category. For example to calculate the exam score in category one (Deception), if the first 4 questions were rated as "Often" (i.e., 3's) and the remaining questions were rated as "Almost Always" (i.e., 4's), the Exam Total would be $(3 + 3 + 3 + 3) + (4 + 4 + 4 + 4 + 4 + 4 + 4)$ = 40/12 = 3.33, rounded off to 3.3 which should be recorded as the complete exam score in the space provided. If any of your Complete Exam Total scores were less than 1.0 or more than 4.0, check your math.

Exam Category	Exam Questions	Category Scores
1. Deception	___ 1, ___ 21, ___ 41, ___ 61, ___81, ___101, ___117, ___136, ___144, ___150, ___158	Category Total ____ /11 = ____
2. Double Standards	___ 2, ___ 22, ___ 42, ___ 62, ___83, ___103, ___118, ___128, ___ 137, ___ 145, ___ 154	Category Total ____ /11 = ____
3. Irresponsible Loyalty	___ 3, ___ 23, ___ 43, ___ 63, ___ 84, ___127	Category Total ____ /6 = ____
4. Don't Care Attitude	___ 4, ___ 24, ___ 44, ___ 64, ___ 85, ___ 105, ___ 119, ___ 129	Category Total ____ /8 = ____
5. Responsibility Issues	___ 6, ___ 26, ___ 46, ___ 66, ___ 87, ___ 97, ___106, ___121, ___ 130, ___ 138, ___ 146, ___ 151, ___ 155, ___ 159	Category Total ____ /14 = ____
6. Blind Ambition	___ 7, ___ 27, ___ 47, ___ 67, ___ 88	Category Total ____ /5 = ____
7. Motivational Blindness	___ 8, ___ 28, ___ 48, ___ 68, ___89, ___107, ___122, ___131, ___ 139, ___ 147, ___ 152	Category Total ____ /11 = ____
8. "I can't" belief	___ 5, ___ 25, ___ 45, ___ 65, ___ 86, ___ 109, ___ 120	Category Total ____ / 7 = ____

Exam Category	Exam Questions	Category Scores
9. Grandiosity	___ 10, ___ 30, ___ 50, ___ 70, ___ 91, ___ 115, ___ 125, ___ 132, ___ 140	Category Total ____/9 = ____
10. Control Issues	___ 9, ___ 29, ___ 49, ___ 69, ___ 90, ___ 108, ___ 123, ___ 133, ___ 141, ___ 148, ___ 153, ___ 156, ___ 160	Category Total ____/13 = ____
11. Image Problems	___ 11, ___ 31, ___ 51, ___ 71, ___ 82, ___ 92, ___ 102, ___ 110, ___ 124, ___ 134, ___ 142, ___ 149, ___ 157	Category Total ____/13 = ____
12. Need Problems	___ 12, ___ 32, ___ 52, ___ 72, ___ 94	Category Total ____/5 = ____
13. Planning Problems	___ 13, ___ 33, ___ 53, ___ 73, ___ 93, ___ 111	Category Total ____/6 = ____
14. Boundary Problems	___ 14, ___ 34, ___ 54, ___ 74, ___ 95, ___ 112, ___ 126, ___ 135, ___ 143	Category Total ____/9 = ____
15. Victim View	___ 16, ___ 36, ___ 56, ___ 76, ___ 96	Category Total ____/5 = ____
16. Justifying Actions	___ 17, ___ 37, ___ 57, ___ 77, ___ 99, ___ 113	Category Total ____/6 = ____
17. Extremism	___ 18, ___ 38, ___ 58, ___ 78, ___ 100, ___ 114	Category Total ____/6 = ____
18. Minimizing	___ 15, ___ 35, ___ 55, ___ 75, ___ 98, ___ 116	Category Total ____/6 = ____
19. Magnifying	___ 20, ___ 40, ___ 60, ___ 80, ___ 104	Category Total ____/5 = ____
20. Assuming	___ 19, ___ 39, ___ 59, ___ 79	Category Total ____/4 = ____
Total Scores	**Exam Score** Add all complete exam category totals & record the result here ____ Divide this total by 160 & record the Exam Score here ____	

Look at each your answers in each category, the closer your answer is to...
- **zero,** the more likely it is that you **never** had this type of thinking or characteristic
- **one,** the more likely it is that you **sometimes** had this type of thinking or characteristic
- **two,** the more likely you had this type of thinking or characteristic **half of the time**
- **three,** the more likely you had this type of thinking or characteristic **often**
- **four,** the more likely you had this type of thinking or characteristic **almost always**

B. Low Score Trouble Shooting: "When you're looking bad, you're looking good"
As was mentioned at the beginning of this exercise, unlike the typical job interview or first date where the object is to "score" highly on making a positive impression, the object of the Awareness and Honesty Exam is to determine how aware you are of shortcomings or problem areas and how honest you are able to be about them. Thus, an overall low score on this exercise which makes you look good in terms of minimal problems, makes you look bad in terms of awareness or honesty and may block the development of an optimal treatment plan for you.

What's normal? The answer depends on whether you are working on changing behaviors that are primarily harmful to self or others. In general, normal ratings for those who have behavioral excesses, go overboard and do something too much are not 0's (Never) or 1's (Sometimes). When dealing with behaviors that are primarily harmful to self, the behavior is likely to be occurring "half the time" (2) or more if it has interfered with your life or required a treatment referral. This is not the case with any behavior that can cause serious harm to self if not changed and this is also not the case when dealing with behaviors that are primarily harmful to others. In cases of danger to self or harm to others "once is enough" to warrant a treatment referral and ratings of 1 (sometimes) on those behaviors reflect a need to seek treatment.

"To thine own self be true" is a 12 Step Recovery Program saying that emphasizes the importance of getting honest with yourself as a first step towards dealing with problems. If you scored below average on this Awareness and Honesty exercise, i.e., have no category ratings at 2.0 (average) or above, and you are completing this exercise because you have been referred for a harmful behavior, a number of factors could have contributed to this low score including…
- You may have simply been reading the questions too fast. Go back through them again taking your time to think about each one to see if that increases any of your rating scores.
- You may have rated many items a "0" or "1" because you don't do them anymore or haven't done them in a long time. Go back and circle all of the item numbers that you did at ANYTIME in your life. Then rate those questions on how often you used to do them.
- You may have simply been reading the questions too literally and should go back through them again to see if your problem rating the question hinges on one or two words. If that is the case, cross those one or two words out and change them to so that you are able to answer in a manner that discloses the problem characteristics that are unique to you and your treatment referral. After making changes to tailor the questions to you, re-rate and re-score the exam to see if you were able to obtain a higher score.
- You may have an Unhealthy Pride image problem that is blocking you from getting honest with others even though you are able to use the mirror concept in treatment, have gained insight from questionnaires and the feedback of others and are aware of the thinking and characteristics that resulted in your referral for treatment. This could require group session work to decrease the social anxiety that comes from getting honest about and let go of problems kept secret in order to free you up to be a more self-confident person. Have others who know your problems rate the 160 questions. Use them as a mirror to see yourself.
- You may have a Motivational Blindness which involves problems seeing yourself as others do and being aware of your motivation (why you do what you do). Motivational blindness

can keep you from using the mirror concept in treatment. The mirror concept involves using the feedback of others as a mirror to see yourself and those who are good at it are also able to use questionnaires to see themselves, gain insight and self-confidence (i.e., develop inner strength through awareness of thinking weaknesses). This could require individual session treatment work to develop your self-awareness to the point where you can identify important thinking problems and characteristics that contributed to your referral for treatment.

- You may have missed information that relates to you. This may be a result of "all or nothing" thinking when rating questions and dropping a rating do to one word that does not apply. Go back and cross out the words that do not apply, write in words that make the statement apply to you but do not change the basic meaning of the statement and then rate it again.

Please consult with your therapist or treatment staff if you have low Awareness and Honesty exam scores, i.e., have no category ratings at 2.0 (average) or above

C. Identify the most frequent the types of past irresponsible thinking listed on your Awareness and Honesty Exam scoring sheet and responsible thinking to substitute.

Follow the structured steps below to write a brief summary of what you discovered about the Irresponsible Thinking and characteristics that supported the problems which led to your treatment referral…

1. Review your Category Scores and circle your top three highest scores.
2. List the top three types of Irresponsible Thinking in order below with the highest score first. If most of the items in one of the Irresponsible Thinking categories that you list below were circled because you did them in the past, write "past" next to that type of Irresponsible Thinking.
3. Look up the definition of each in Appendix C, page 94. Since each Irresponsible Thinking type includes a broad category of characteristics, underline the parts that apply to you and write the characteristics of each type of Irresponsible Thinking that you underlined below. Then write an example of responsible thinking that you need to substitute if or when this type of irresponsible thinking hits you again (Hint: Try to use your own words but if you need to get some ideas, review your healthy relationship and behavior success skills on page 10- 16 along with the basic category examples are in Appendix C).

Irresponsible Thinking Type #1 _____ Score = ___ Label = _____

Characteristics of this type of thinking that I have- _____

_____

Responsible Thinking #1, What I can say to myself to avoid this type of irresponsible thinking-

_____

Irresponsible Thinking Type #2 _____ Score = ___ Label = _____

Characteristics of this type of thinking that I have- _____

_____

Responsible Thinking #2, What I can say to myself to avoid this type of irresponsible thinking-

_____

Irresponsible Thinking Type #3 _____ Score = ___ Label = _____

Characteristics of this type of thinking that I have- _____

_____

Responsible Thinking #3, What I can say to myself to avoid this type of irresponsible thinking-

_____

Which of the above types of irresponsible thinking listed above do you believe had the strongest impact on you and led to your treatment referral? List your personal quotes (i.e., self-statements, things you would say to yourself such as "It's not that bad")

Personal Quote #1 _____

_____

Personal Quote #2 _____

_____

Personal Quote #3 _____

_____

D. Irresponsible Thinking Before, During and After your referral target behavior

Record the unhealthy, harmful behavior that resulted in your referral for treatment and is the primary target behavior you need to change (disclosed on page 4) in the space provided below. Then see if you can discover your irresponsible thinking before, during and after your referral target behavior. (Hint: Look at your high exam question and category scores on your Awareness and Honesty Examination Scoring Sheet. Then review your most frequent Irresponsible Thinking and the personal quotes that you listed in section C above. If you are in a treatment group or have a therapist get their opinion.)

Target behavior (that resulted in referral for treatment) _____

Irresponsible Thinking Before the behavior:_____

_____

Irresponsible Thinking During the behavior: _____

_____

Irresponsible Thinking After the behavior: _____

_____

What can you do about it: Responsible Self-statement Substitution 101

Irresponsible self-statements are things that you say to yourself that support unhealthy, harmful behavior. Responsible self-statements are things that you say to yourself that support healthy, helpful behavior and keeps you from falling back into problem behavior. Responsible self-statement substitution is just learning how to talk to yourself like your own best friend. Examples are listed in Appendix C (p. 94).While others may want to work you up for their own selfish reasons, best friends want the best for you. Instead of trying to work you up, best friends try to talk you down. They help you avoid trouble, calm down think it through and solve the problem.

If you were standing next to your best friend in the whole world when something bad happened, they would ask you how you are doing and then try to offer you some thoughts that would help make things better instead of worse. They would help you substitute any irresponsible thinking you were having that could cause problems for you with responsible thoughts to help you avoid problems. Since you can't always be standing next to your best friend in the whole world when bad things happen, you have to learn to listen to what you are saying to yourself and then talk to yourself like your own best friend. To do this you have to become aware of irresponsible thoughts when they hit and substitute responsible thinking in order to avoid falling back into problems. Doing this takes practice. Your Situation, Response, Analysis Log explained in section E below will help you learn to talk to yourself like your own best friend.

Use the space below to explain how you could use responsible self-statement substitution or any of your healthy relationship and behavior success skills (page 10- 16) to help you change your irresponsible thinking in the following three situations. (If you are in a treatment group or have a therapist discuss this with them.) Pay very close attention to justifying actions based on feelings, minimizing and blaming because these irresponsible thoughts are strong relapse triggers (See Link 4, p. 84).   **Explain what you need to do when...**

1. you are thinking about doing your problem behavior _____

   _____

   _____

   _____

2. you have started to do your problem behavior _____

   _____

   _____

   _____

3. you have done your problem behavior again _____

   _____

   _____

   _____

E. Begin using your Situation Response Analysis Log

This log was designed to increase your self-awareness of the Irresponsible Thinking that you use on everyday problem situations. Make time to sit down every evening to review your day and record events in your log. The Situation Response Analysis Log and instructions are provided for you in Appendix D, p. 107. Be sure to make at least one log entry every day as you will be using what you learned from this log in your treatment sessions and later in workbook 3. Use this log as a way to become more aware of your thoughts feelings and behavior in difficult situations. Don't forget to record using your **healthy relationship and behavior success skills** on page 10-16 when you use them for Positive Coping in a problem situation. Consult with your therapist or staff about whether you should complete the Candy Bar Exercise in Appendix D to develop Irresponsible Thinking awareness. (Hint: Don't put your name on logs until you turn them in so if you lose a log you can't be identified).

F. Irresponsible Thinking Structured Discovery Exercise #1

Identify the types of Irresponsible Thinking that you believe triggered your target behavior by looking for connections between your most frequent Irresponsible thinking (section C, p. 65) and your thinking before during and after your target behavior (section D, p. 66). Circle any similarities that you find and use these connections to discover all of the types of Irresponsible Thinking that led to your referral target behavior. List the types of Irresponsible Thinking that were triggers for your target behavior in the space provide below. For example, suppose you listed your thinking before your target behavior as "I'll only do this once", during the behavior as "What I am doing is not that bad" and after the behavior as "No big deal, others do it to". In addition, suppose that your Irresponsible Thinking category 18 scores were high compared to your scores in the other categories and you listed "Minimizing" as one of your top three most frequent types of Irresponsible Thinking. You would circle these connections and list "Minimizing" below as one of the strongest triggers of your target behavior.

_____

_____

_____

Link #4 Summary Completion Instructions- Record at least the top three types of Irresponsible Thinking that led to your target behavior referral **on the Risk Factor Chain worksheet (page 81)** at the end of this section (use the second page "continued" portion of your worksheet if needed). Imagine yourself teaching someone else about this part of your life. Put your important descriptions in phrase form that makes it easy for you to explain and makes sense when read by others. Don't limit yourself to the top three points if there are important parts that fit in this area. Make sure that you do not leave out any important information on this topic and be sure to include what you can do about it. Use margins if needed.

Get honest about your Irresponsible Thinking. Discuss the top three types of Irresponsible Thinking that led to your referral target behavior with your therapist or group if you are in treatment. Log your discussion in the space provided below.

Date: _____ Discussed with: _____

The Risk Factor Chain: LINK #5- Initial Harmful Behavior
(Cumulative impact of risk factors)

"Having the tools to change your life and succeed in recovery means nothing if you don't choose to use those tools. Using those tools is tough, but the alternative is tougher" -- Edward Flowers (1934- 2008)

Name: _____   **Date:** _____

Definition: The Initial Harmful Behavior occurs in Link #5 where all of the risk factors we reviewed accumulate or add up to set the occasion for a harmful behavior or episode. Harmful behavior occurs when irresponsible thinking (e.g., minimizing, justifying, assuming) is used in high risk situations (e.g., exposure to trigger feelings, people or places) before you have developed the emotional maturity to deal with it (i.e., awareness of trouble is brewing, confidence in handling the situation and self-control to do the right thing) which results in poor judgment, uncontrolled emotional urges and actions that are harmful to self or others. The motivation behind this socially irresponsible behavior typically involves trying to feel better (i.e., elevate mood, feel in control, confident) or get relief (decrease negative feelings of helplessness, anxiety, anger).

Risk Factor Question #5: What links do you see between the risk factors we have discussed and your harmful behavior?

About Harmful behavior: Nobody is perfect, everybody makes mistakes
Good people have good values but they are not perfect. Values are the goals we shoot for in terms of how we want to be. How good we are at making those goals, sticking to our values being who we want to be and "doing the right thing" is a different matter. In Social Responsibility Therapy, doing the right thing is sticking to our healthy relationship success skills by being honest, trustworthy, loyal, concerned and responsible.

Everybody makes mistakes. Lots of people value honesty, trust, loyalty, concern and responsibility but make mistakes and fall into back into unhealthy, harmful behavior. Mistakes with values can lead to falling into unhealthy, harmful behavior. For example...
- Mistakes on honesty by exaggerating can lead to falling back into lying.
- Mistakes on trusting others by keeping things to yourself can lead to falling back into secret keeping about unhealthy, harmful behavior and staying by yourself.
- Mistakes on being trustworthy by borrowing without asking can lead to falling back into stealing.
- Mistakes on loyalty by not telling your partner who you are visiting can lead to falling into relationship cheating.
- Mistakes on concern for yourself by hanging with negative peers can lead to falling back into unhealthy smoking, eating, drinking or drugging with them.
- Mistakes on concern for others by dwelling on angry or arousing thoughts can lead to falling back into harmful physical or sexual behavior.
- Mistakes on personal responsibility by not coming forward with mistakes can lead to falling back into blaming others.

- Mistakes on social responsibility by not thinking about how your actions could affect others can lead to falling back into a "don't care" attitude and giving up on self-control.

Use the space below to write an example of how a mistake on honesty, trust, loyalty, concern or responsibility led you to taking a fall into unhealthy, harmful behavior.

_____

_____

_____

In making mistakes and falling back into unhealthy, harmful behavior, how quickly you get back up is more important than how many mistakes you make. What really matters is how quickly you can get back on your feet and on back on the right track. Every minute you stay down is another minute you hurt yourself or others. Every minute you stand and stay on track with your values after a fall is another minute you reclaim your dignity through your honesty, trust, loyalty, concern and responsibility.

A. Awareness and Honesty Examination #2

The following is a brief exam to help you see how you have become more aware and honest about your unhealthy, harmful behavior since you first started this workbook.

Please indicate all of the UNHEALTHY, HARMFUL THINGS that <u>you have done to yourself</u> in the following section.

Read each statement carefully. If you **have not done** the harmful behavior described, **mark an "X"** in front of the statement. If you **have done** the behavior described, underline the part that you did and **rate how harmful** or damaging you believe **it was TO YOURSELF**.

0 Not Harmful to myself at all	1 A little Harmful to myself	2 Moderately Harmful	3 Highly Harmful to myself	4 Extremely Harmful

___ 1) Regular tobacco use, e.g., cigarettes, cigars, chewing tobacco, other (_____)

___ 2) Drinking too much, alcohol over use or abuse

___ 3) Drug abuse, e.g., marijuana, stimulants (cocaine, amphetamine), narcotics/opiates

(heroin), other (_____)

___ 4) Prescription drug abuse (<u>List type(s)-</u>_____)

___ 5) Quitting school

___ 6) Quitting one job without getting another one first

___ 7) Weight gain from regular overeating, regular junk food eating or binge eating

___ 8) Making myself throw up (for weight loss)

___ 9) Abusing laxatives (for weight loss)

If you **have not done** the harmful behavior described, **mark an "X"** in front of the statement. If you **have done** the behavior described, underline the part that you did and **rate how harmful** or damaging you believe **it was TO YOURSELF**.

0 Not Harmful to myself at all	1 A little Harmful to myself	2 Moderately Harmful	3 Highly Harmful to myself	4 Extremely Harmful

___ 10) Exercise abuse (i.e., to the point where it causes health or life problems)

___ 11) Nutritional self-abuse (starving self/not eating on purpose)

___ 12) Acting hurt, hurting yourself or doing things wrong to try and make others feel bad, guilty and stay with you or give you extra attention.

___ 13) Self-mutilation, hurting self (e.g., cutting self, pulling hair out)

___ 14) Suicide attempt

___ 15) Verbal self abuse (self punishment and put downs)

___ 16) Excessive/compulsive sexual activity- sexual acting out, promiscuous sex, too much sex with consenting partners of same age group (e.g., many partners, partner swapping, phone sex, compulsive masturbation, constant sex preoccupation)

___ 17) Cruising (the internet, bars, clubs or the street) for sexual opportunities or prostitutes

___ 18) Compromising yourself to be accepted (having sex to avoid being alone, feeling lonely)

___ 18) Prostituting self (sex for money), having sex for drugs, having sex for a place to stay

___ 20) Unprotected sex with strangers

___ 21) Having sex with prostitutes

___ 22) Pornography over use or abuse

___ 23) Money abuse (check➔ __over spending, __shopaholic, __credit card abuse)

___ 24) Getting in debt or gambling debt

___ 25) Committing crimes for the "thrill"

___ 26) Getting arrested for doing things that I knew I shouldn't

___ 27) Associating with addicts or known criminals

___ 28) Staying in abusive or destructive relationships

___ 29) Quitting or leaving relationships for no good reason

___ 30) Serial relationships, one after another just to have someone and not be alone

___ 31) Going back to bad, unfaithful, controlling, harmful or abusive relationships

___ 32) Other behavior that has been harmful to yourself (List- _____)

B. Please indicate all of the UNHEALTHY, HARMFUL THINGS that <u>you have done to others</u> in the following section.

Read each statement carefully.

If you **have not done** the harmful behavior described below, **mark an "X"** in front of the statement.

If you **have done** the behavior described, underline the part that you did and **rate how harmful** or damaging you believe **it was TO OTHERS**.

0 Not Harmful to others at all	1 A little Harmful to others	2 Moderately Harmful	3 Highly Harmful to others	4 Extremely Harmful

___ 1) Dealing/selling drugs (<u>List-</u>_____).

___ 2) Drunk driving or other reckless, dangerous behavior.

___ 3) Responsibility neglect- Letting your responsibilities go and just doing what you want, what is easiest, what you feel like doing or what makes you feel good at the time (Youth example- making excuses to miss or skip school/work, not completing activities that are required of you; Adult example- failure to pay bills, being an absent parent to your children, compulsive, excessive exercise or caught up in relationship to the point where family/job are let go (see Planning Problems p. 102).

___ 4) Responsibility abuse- Refusal to accept your responsibilities (Includes irresponsible behavior, for example quitting school or job training, quitting a job without getting another job first. Also includes pathological priorities, for example as a parent putting involvement in adult relationships/activities before family/child care needs (see p. 97- 98)

___ 5) Loyalty neglect such as: walking out on a friend in need; shifting your loyalties to others when it seems to benefit you or when things aren't going well for your current friends or; putting associates before family.

___ 6) Loyalty abuse- Ignoring long time friends and showing favoritism to associates who are more attractive and popular or as a parent by spending more time with one child than another.

___ 7) Trust abuse (i.e., abusing the trust of others by lying, deceiving, manipulating, conning, coercion, fraud, running away, child neglect, encapsulating self in partner or work/workaholic and neglecting family, having affairs, cheating on a partner or having an intimate relationship with more than one person while telling them both what they want to hear).

___ 8) Concern (or emotional) abuse, e.g. putting others down to build yourself up or being cruel and hurting others emotionally to get power over them or to win a sick argument (e.g., spitting on someone while insulting them).

___ 9) Power abuse (i.e., using your position of status, popularity or power to get others to do what you want- winning by intimidation, controlling/dominating).

If you **have not done** the harmful behavior described below, **mark an "X"** in front of the statement. If you **have done** the behavior described, underline the part that you did and **rate how harmful** or damaging you believe **it was TO OTHERS**.

0 Not Harmful to others at all	1 A little Harmful to others	2 Moderately Harmful to others	3 Highly Harmful to others	4 Extremely Harmful to others

___ 10) Emotional neglect (e.g., refusal to offer comfort and support to another person that you can see is hurting and needs help or giving those who care about you the "silent treatment").

___ 11) Physical neglect (e.g., not sharing when asked or not giving something that you don't really need to someone who needs it more).

___ 12) Taken advantage of someone's weakness to get your own way.

___ 13) Verbal abuse (e.g., threats of violence- to hit, beat up, stab, shoot, kill- with severe temper, rageaholic).

___ 14) Property abuse (i.e., theft, shoplifting, vandalism, arson, forgery, black mail or extortion (getting money by threats), borrowing without permission, borrowing and not returning things).

___ 15) Physical abuse (e.g., assault, kidnapping, robbery, school bullying, physical intimidation, child physical abuse/toxic parenting/excessive corporal punishment, held down, pushed, shoved, slapped, hit, assault with a deadly weapon, stabbed, shot someone- including hitting, slapping a partner during arguments- also includes conviction on domestic violence or disorderly conduct from fighting).

___ 16) Sexual harassment, sexual coercion (talking someone into it), exhibitionism/flashing, voyeurism/peeping, pandering/pimping (getting someone to sell themselves for sex)

___ 17) Sexual abuse of someone your age or an adult (e.g., rape, coerced or forced them into sexual acts or got them drunk/high so you could take advantage of them sexually or getting others to prostitute themselves).

___ 18) Sexual abuse of a child (i.e., any type of sexual contact with a child under age 13 or sexual contact with someone under age 18 who was 5 or more years younger than you).

___ 19) Homicide or homicide attempt (violent assault with intent to kill).

___ 20) Other behavior that has been harmful to others (List- _____)

C. List the top three types of unhealthy, harmful behavior that you did to yourself or others on the chart provided. Then estimate: how long you have had this problem (in years and months or from what age to what age), how frequently you have engaged in it (times per day, week, month) and the rating you gave it on how serious the problem is or could be in terms of being harmful and/or destructive. Circle the harmful behavior that you have done most frequently and your most serious harmful behavior.

Type of unhealthy, harmful behavior List top 3 behaviors that were harmful to self or others	How long you had this problem (years & months) If stopped, list when you stopped	How often you did it (times per day, week, month)	How serious it was (1- 5 rating, 5= very serious)
Harmful to self			
1-			
2-			
3-			
Harmful to others			
1-			
2-			
3-			

D. **Review the top three types of harmful behavior that you did to yourself and others in the chart above.**

How did you usually feel during these behaviors that were harmful to self & others?	What did you usually say to yourself to make it easier for you to do these things? (Hint look at your answers on page 65- 66)
Harmful to self (list behavior & feelings)	(list behavior & thoughts)
1- Feelings-	1- Thoughts-
2- Feelings-	2- Thoughts-
3- Feelings-	3- Thoughts-
Harmful to others	
1- Feelings-	1- Thoughts-
2- Feelings-	2- Thoughts-
3- Feelings-	3- Thoughts-

E. Review the top three: <u>upsetting</u> things that <u>happened to you</u> in the past (i.e., from LINK #1, Section A- E, p. 21- 26); **unhealthy, harmful things that you have <u>done to yourself</u>** (i.e., from LINK #5, Section A, p. 70- 71); **unhealthy, harmful things that you have <u>done to others</u>** (i.e., from LINK #5, Section B, p. 72- 73) **and**

List the similarities between what was done to you, what you did to yourself and what you did to others. What similar behavior, thoughts and feelings do you see in these situations?

_____

_____

_____

_____

(If you need more space, use the workspace on page 79, 116 or the inside of the front and back covers)

F. Link #5 Summary Completion Instructions- Review your answers to Link #5, Section C (p. 73- 74) on behavior seriousness and frequency. Then record:
- the target harmful behavior that resulted in your treatment referral;
- your #1 most SERIOUS harmful behavior that you did to self or others;
- your #1 most FREQUENT harmful behavior that you did to self or others;

as your three types of Initial Harmful Behavior. Then record these on the Risk Factor Chain worksheet (page 81) at the end of this section.

Go back over the unhealthy, harmful behaviors that you have done and answer the following three questions. If you are in treatment discuss these questions with your group or therapist.

1. Is your target referral behavior the most SERIOUS behavior you have ever been involved with? __Yes; __No (List the most serious _____).

2. Is your target referral behavior the most FREQUENT behavior you have done in the past? __Yes; __No (List the harmful behavior you did the most _____).

3. Was your target referral behavior the first unhealthy, harmful behavior you ever did? __Yes; __No (List the first unhealthy, harmful behavior you did and how old you were

_____).

   If you answered "No" to any of these three questions, what can you do to avoid falling back into the other harmful behaviors that you listed? (Hint: what ACTS skills have you learned?)

_____

_____

G. Review of your Healthy Relationship Success Skills Progress
The following is a review of your progress in developing your healthy relationship success skills (p. 11) since you started this workbook. Go over the harmful behaviors you recorded on pages 4- 6 and compare it to your work in this section.

Honesty: What other harmful behavior did you get honest about? _____

_____

Trust: Who did you trust with this information? _____

Loyalty: Have you been loyal by standing up for what you know is right by it and not going

along with unhealthy, harmful behavior? Give an example _____

_____

Concern: Have you helped yourself by working on you target behavior problem? Give an

example _____

Have you helped others? Give an example _____

Responsibility: Have you been responsible by using you ACTS skills and holding on to self-

control? Give an example _____

_____

H. Update your relapse prevention plan (p. 51) with your therapist or treatment staff for
your referral form of harmful behavior (behavior that resulted in your treatment referral)
based on what you have learned from your Risk Factor Chain. Make sure you add:

1. Historical Risk Factors including tough things that you experienced in the past that could set
you up for relapse if you got caught up in them;

2. Social-Emotional Risk Factors including important social maturity factors (problems with
honesty, trust, loyalty, concern and responsibility) and emotional maturity factors (being
aware of what is going on with your thoughts, mood and surroundings, confidence to face
problems and self-control to handle them in the right way) that could set you up for relapse;

3. Situational Risk Factors including people, places and emotions that could set you up for
relapse if you got caught up in them;

4. Cognitive Risk Factors including the thoughts before during and after your harmful behavior
that could set you up for relapse if you got caught up in them.

I. Begin your promise letter. Use the important Risk Factor Chain information that you
became aware of to begin a promise letter to the significant others in your life (and/or to
yourself if you keep letting yourself down) explaining your understanding of your problem
thus far, how you are going to use that knowledge in your relapse prevention plan along with
your commitment to change. Start with "Dear (list name of parent, partner, peer, etc.) and
others I have let down in my life", and continue with something to the effect of- "I am
making a commitment to stop (the harmful behavior) that led to my need for treatment. I
have learned about how I acquired this problem and would like to share that with you. In my
case, The Risk Factor Chain that led to my (harmful behavior) involved..." and explain what
you have learned from this workbook. Keep the focus on the present and your behavior (not
the past and others) along with your risk factor understanding and relapse prevention
knowledge (p. 84).

"Two heads are better than one, four eyes are better than two". If you are in treatment, discuss your relapse prevention plan and promise letter with your therapist or treatment group. In all of your Social Responsibility Therapy discussions, use the "Window Concept" to help you decide what to apply and the "Mirror Concept" to help you accept and benefit most from what applies. The "Window Concept" involves keeping the window open by keeping an open mind, taking in everything everyone tells you and examining it carefully. If it is helpful to yourself or others hold it dear to your heart, if it's not, shovel it out the window. If there is any doubt about whether to keep and apply the feedback you receive, use group consensus (i.e., "If ten people say you're a horse, you're a horse"). The "Mirror Concept" holds that "other people see you better than you see yourself" and you need to use their feedback as a mirror to get a better view of yourself. Use feedback to improve your relapse prevention plan, your promise letter and your self-awareness.

Risk Factor Chain Conclusion- The Risk Factor Chain is a very simple concept. It starts with a Link 1 **can** (made of historical stressors) which gets filled with Link 2 **gasoline** (social maturity problems and unwanted feelings) and placed near a Link 3 **spark** (high risk situation that triggers trouble) using Link 4 irresponsible thinking (minimizing or rationalizing why it's OK to do that risky behavior or stay in that risky situation) that creates a Link 5 **behavior explosion** (unhealthy, harmful behavior).

The saying that "If you forget where you come from, you're doomed to return there" applies to individuals with harmful behavior who have been abstinent (problem free) for a period of time and lose touch with where they came from in terms of having to keep their problem up front as a continuing life priority. Individuals with harmful behavior who forget where they came from and allow other issues to take priority over their past harmful behavior issues have let down their guard. Since they are not taking appropriate care of themselves, they are doomed to eventually fall back into their Stress-Relapse Cycle and return to harmful behavior.

Completing your Harmful Behavior Time Line- Since "a picture is worth a thousand words", mapping out all of the harmful behavior that was done to you and that you did to yourself or others on a time line will help you see the connections between your past and your behavior. Complete the Harmful Behavior Time line in Appendix F. (p. 112) and use the connections you discover to complete your harmful behavior life impact statement below.

Life Impact Statement: The Risk Factor Chain- Use the space below to record how the harmful behavior that resulted in your referral for treatment: has affected your life; what it has done to yourself and others; where it has put you; how it has held you back; where you would like to be at this point in your life and; what you can do about it now. End by describing your life five years from now if things work out for you.

_____

_____

_____

_____

_____

_____

_____

_____

_____

_____

_____

_____

_____

_____

_____

_____

_____

_____

(If you need more space, use the workspace on page 79, 116 or the inside of the front and back covers)

Discuss the impact that your harmful behavior has had on yourself and others with your therapist or group if you are in treatment. Write a brief summary of the harmful life impact that you recorded above next to the Link #5 box under your name and date on the Risk Factor Chain worksheet at the end of this section (page 81). Now go back and update your referral behavior history (p. 6) with what you have learned about yourself.

Congratulations! You have now completed your work on understanding how you acquired or developed your harmful behavior through "The Risk Factor Chain". Make a presentation to your treatment group or therapist on how you developed your harmful behavior.

Complete your Social Responsibility Therapy self-evaluation using the form provided in Appendix E, p. 111. If you are in treatment, discuss your evaluation with your therapist or group.

The Next Step. A pattern of harmful behavior wasn't developed overnight and understanding it won't be developed overnight either. It takes a great deal of work to understand "The Problem Development Triad" on how you got the problem, what kept it going and how it spread to other life areas. Developing an understanding of "How did I get this problem?" is an important step in reclaiming your dignity through honesty about the thoughts, feelings and motivations that led to your unhealthy, harmful behavior. Those that continue on the social responsibility path to develop an understanding of "Why do I keep doing this?" will move another step closer towards finding themselves, a place in the world where they can be themselves and the fulfillment of a positive lifestyle that is free of unhealthy, harmful behavior.

Workspace (Label your work)

"Every small, positive change we can make in ourselves repays us in confidence in the future"- Alice Walker

_____
_____
_____
_____
_____
_____
_____
_____
_____
_____
_____
_____
_____
_____
_____
_____
_____
_____
_____
_____
_____
_____
_____
_____
_____
_____
_____
_____

Workspace (Label your work)   "The best vision is insight"--Malcolm Forbes (1917-1990)

The Risk Factor Chain Worksheet- How Harmful Behavior was Acquired:
The Risk Factor Chain that led to unhealthy, harmful behavior

Name:

_____

Date:

_____

Initial Unhealthy Harmful Behavior (from interaction of all risk factors resulting in underdeveloped social-emotional maturity)

Cognitive Risk Factors (Irresponsible Thinking)

Situational Risk Factors (High Risk Situations)

Not your responsibility then

Social-Emotional Risk Factors (Social & emotional maturity problems)

Note: <u>Social maturity</u>= honesty, trust, loyalty, concern & responsibility; <u>Emotional maturity</u>= self-awareness, self-efficacy & self-control.

Your responsibility now

Historical Risk Factors (Past traumatic events or things that created permanent problems)

Note: Includes biopsychosocial problems, physical, social, emotional trauma history & other predisposing factors

Risk Factor Chain Worksheet (continued)

Initial Unhealthy, Harmful Behavior (continued): _____

_____

_____

_____

_____

Cognitive Risk Factors (Irresponsible thinking)- continued: _____

_____

_____

_____

_____

Situational Risk Factors (High risk situations)- continued: _____

_____

_____

_____

_____

Social-Emotional Risk Factors (Problems with social maturity- honesty, trust, loyalty, concern, responsibility and emotional maturity- self-awareness, self-confidence, self-control)- continued:

_____

_____

_____

_____

Historical Risk Factors (Past personal problems continued): _____

_____

_____

_____

_____

Footnotes

1. Adapted by Research Engineer Russell Yokley for practical problems from 1968 San Francisco speech by Eldridge Cleaver (1935- present, American Black Leader, Writer), "What we're saying today is that you're either part of the solution or you're part of the problem".

2. The healthy behavior success skills utilized were drawn from the following four research-supported intervention areas: Relapse Prevention; Emotional Regulation; Decisional Balance and; Social Problem Solving.

3. Further information is provided in Yokley (2008) on: Avoid trouble (relapse prevention)- p. 154- 155; Calm down (emotional regulation)- p. 157- 160; Think it through (decisional balance)- p. 165- 166; Solve the problem (social problem solving)- p. 156. Therapist guide on developing healthy behavior success skills is provided in Yokley (2010)

4. The ABC's used here were condensed from the Rational Emotive Behavior Therapy (REBT) developed by Dr. Albert Ellis. See Ellis & Bernard (2006) for further description of the REBT approach with children and Ellis & Velten (1992) for further description of REBT with adults exhibiting harmful, addictive behavior.

5. From The Life of Reason, Vol. 1, 1905, George Santayana (1863- 1952, American Philosopher, Poet).

References

Ellis, A., & Bernard, M. E. (Eds.). (2006). *Rational emotive behavioral approaches to childhood disorders: Theory, practice and research.* New York, NY: Springer Science & Business Media Inc.

Ellis, A., & Velten, E. (1992). *When AA doesn't work for you: Rational steps to quitting alcohol.* Fort Lee, New Jersey: Barricade Books, Inc.

Yokley, J. (2008). *Social Responsibility Therapy for Adolescents & Young Adults: A Multicultural Treatment Manual for Harmful Behavior,* New York, NY, US: Routledge/Taylor & Francis Group. www.routledgementalhealth.com

Yokley, J. (in press). *The Clinician's Guide to Social Responsibility Therapy: Practical Applications, Theory and Research Support.* North Myrtle Beach, SC: Social Solutions Press.

Yokley, J. & Dudich, J. (in press). *Social Responsibility Therapy for Preteen Children: A Multicultural Treatment Manual for Harmful Behavior.* Bloomington, Indiana: Trafford Publishing. www.srtonline.org

Exhibit 1.
Managing Risk Factors for How Harmful Behavior was Acquired:
The Risk Factor Chain (that led to harmful behavior, i.e., biopsychosocial risk factors)
(Summary of risk factor coping skills in Workbook 1)

Note: A more complete set of "Treatment Notes" with case examples for each one of these categories is provided in "Understanding Harmful Behavior: A Social Responsibility Therapy Perspective." www.srtonline.org.

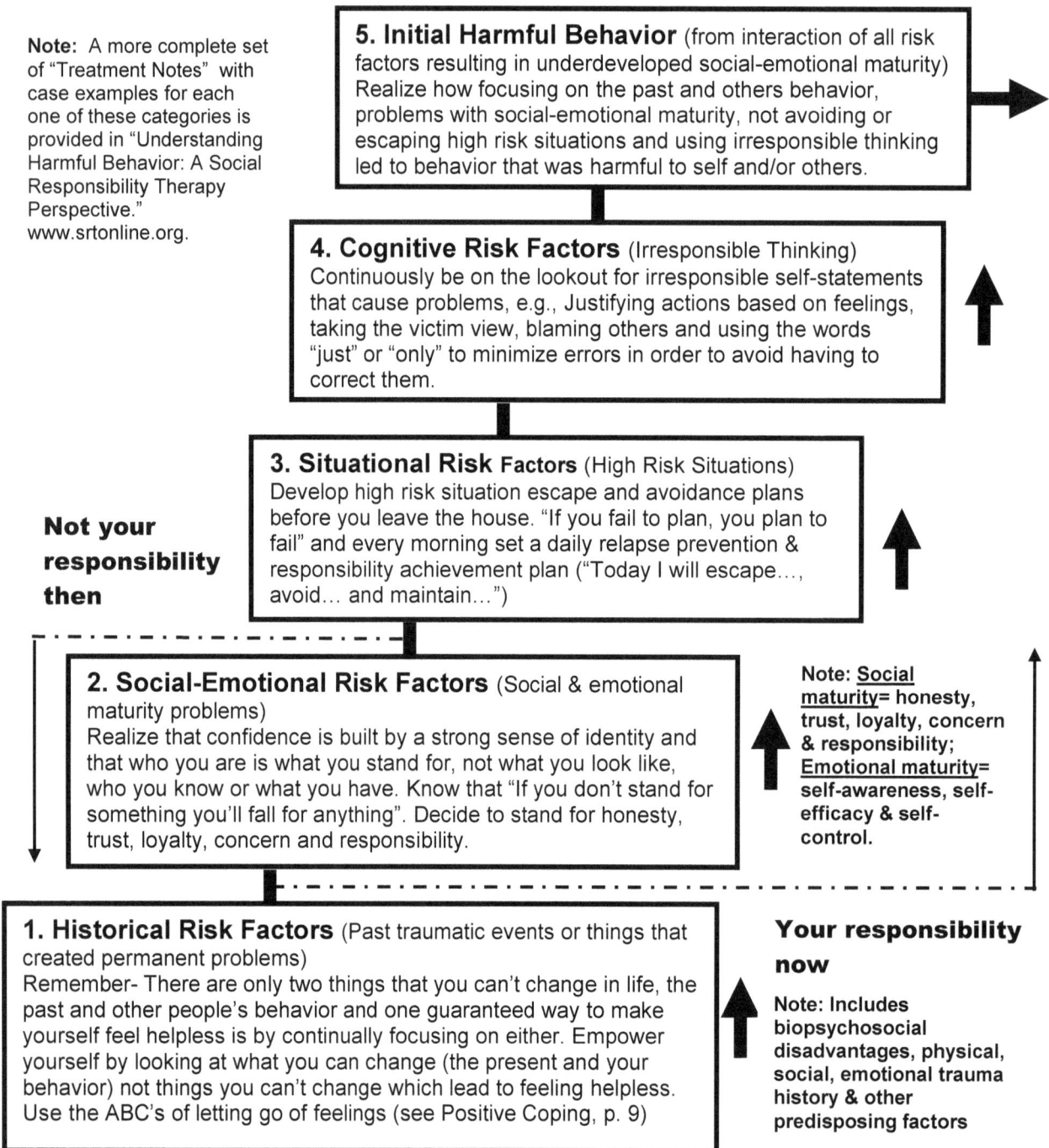

5. Initial Harmful Behavior (from interaction of all risk factors resulting in underdeveloped social-emotional maturity) Realize how focusing on the past and others behavior, problems with social-emotional maturity, not avoiding or escaping high risk situations and using irresponsible thinking led to behavior that was harmful to self and/or others.

4. Cognitive Risk Factors (Irresponsible Thinking) Continuously be on the lookout for irresponsible self-statements that cause problems, e.g., Justifying actions based on feelings, taking the victim view, blaming others and using the words "just" or "only" to minimize errors in order to avoid having to correct them.

3. Situational Risk Factors (High Risk Situations) Develop high risk situation escape and avoidance plans before you leave the house. "If you fail to plan, you plan to fail" and every morning set a daily relapse prevention & responsibility achievement plan ("Today I will escape…, avoid… and maintain…")

Not your responsibility then

2. Social-Emotional Risk Factors (Social & emotional maturity problems) Realize that confidence is built by a strong sense of identity and that who you are is what you stand for, not what you look like, who you know or what you have. Know that "If you don't stand for something you'll fall for anything". Decide to stand for honesty, trust, loyalty, concern and responsibility.

Note: Social maturity= honesty, trust, loyalty, concern & responsibility; Emotional maturity= self-awareness, self-efficacy & self-control.

1. Historical Risk Factors (Past traumatic events or things that created permanent problems) Remember- There are only two things that you can't change in life, the past and other people's behavior and one guaranteed way to make yourself feel helpless is by continually focusing on either. Empower yourself by looking at what you can change (the present and your behavior) not things you can't change which lead to feeling helpless. Use the ABC's of letting go of feelings (see Positive Coping, p. 9)

Your responsibility now

Note: Includes biopsychosocial disadvantages, physical, social, emotional trauma history & other predisposing factors

Exhibit 2.
Recovery Behavior Maintenance: The Stress Management Cycle (that maintains appropriate social behavior control and develops social-emotional maturity)
(Summary of stress management skills from Workbook 2)

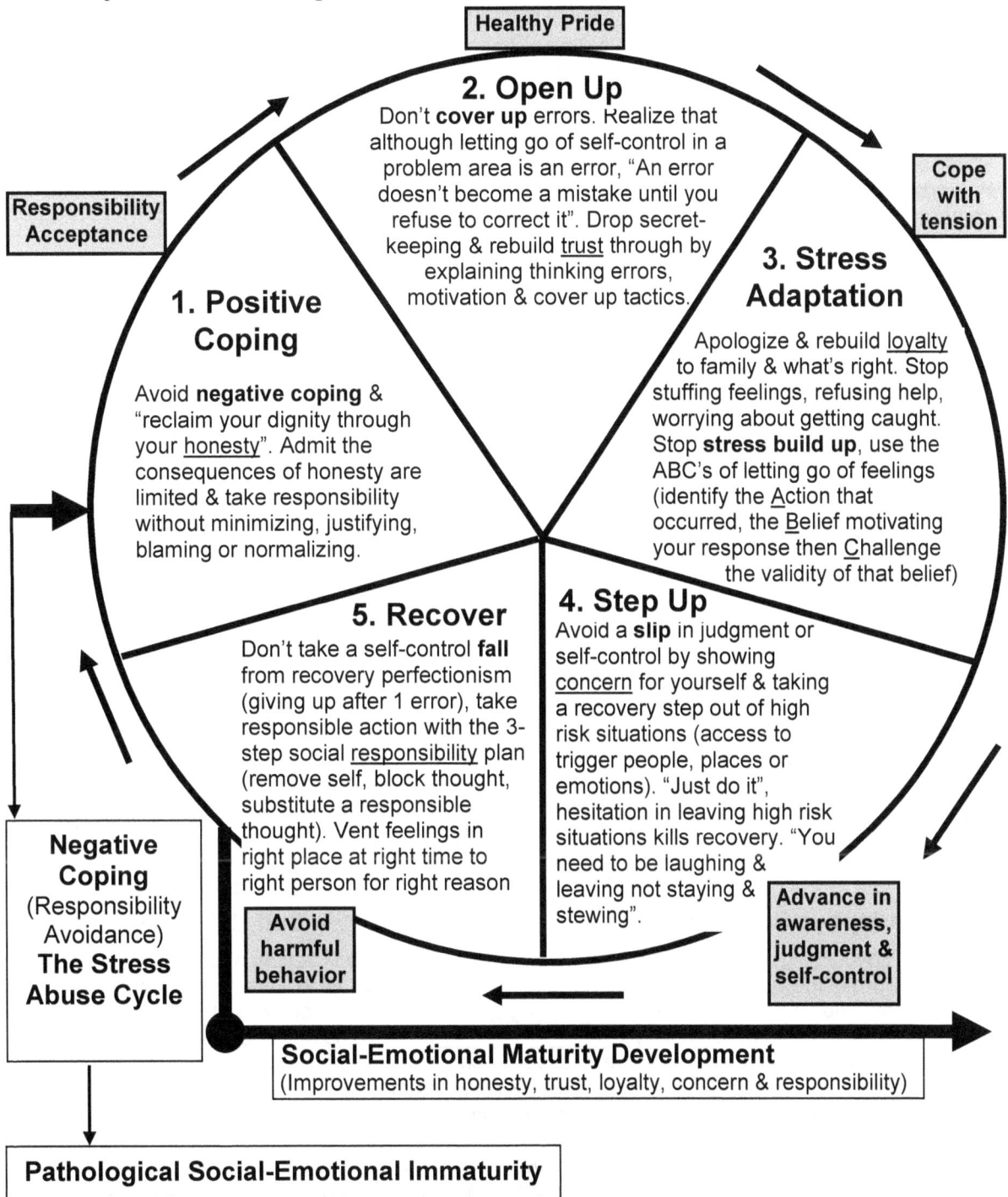

Healthy Pride

2. Open Up
Don't **cover up** errors. Realize that although letting go of self-control in a problem area is an error, "An error doesn't become a mistake until you refuse to correct it". Drop secret-keeping & rebuild <u>trust</u> through by explaining thinking errors, motivation & cover up tactics.

Responsibility Acceptance

Cope with tension

1. Positive Coping

Avoid **negative coping** & "reclaim your dignity through your <u>honesty</u>". Admit the consequences of honesty are limited & take responsibility without minimizing, justifying, blaming or normalizing.

3. Stress Adaptation

Apologize & rebuild <u>loyalty</u> to family & what's right. Stop stuffing feelings, refusing help, worrying about getting caught. Stop **stress build up**, use the ABC's of letting go of feelings (identify the <u>A</u>ction that occurred, the <u>B</u>elief motivating your response then <u>C</u>hallenge the validity of that belief)

5. Recover
Don't take a self-control **fall** from recovery perfectionism (giving up after 1 error), take responsible action with the 3-step social <u>responsibility</u> plan (remove self, block thought, substitute a responsible thought). Vent feelings in right place at right time to right person for right reason

4. Step Up
Avoid a **slip** in judgment or self-control by showing <u>concern</u> for yourself & taking a recovery step out of high risk situations (access to trigger people, places or emotions). "Just do it", hesitation in leaving high risk situations kills recovery. "You need to be laughing & leaving not staying & stewing".

Avoid harmful behavior

Advance in awareness, judgment & self-control

Negative Coping (Responsibility Avoidance) **The Stress Abuse Cycle**

Social-Emotional Maturity Development
(Improvements in honesty, trust, loyalty, concern & responsibility)

Pathological Social-Emotional Immaturity

Exhibit 3. Addressing Factors that Support Multiple forms of Harmful Behavior[1]
(Summary of prosocial behavior skills from Workbook 3)

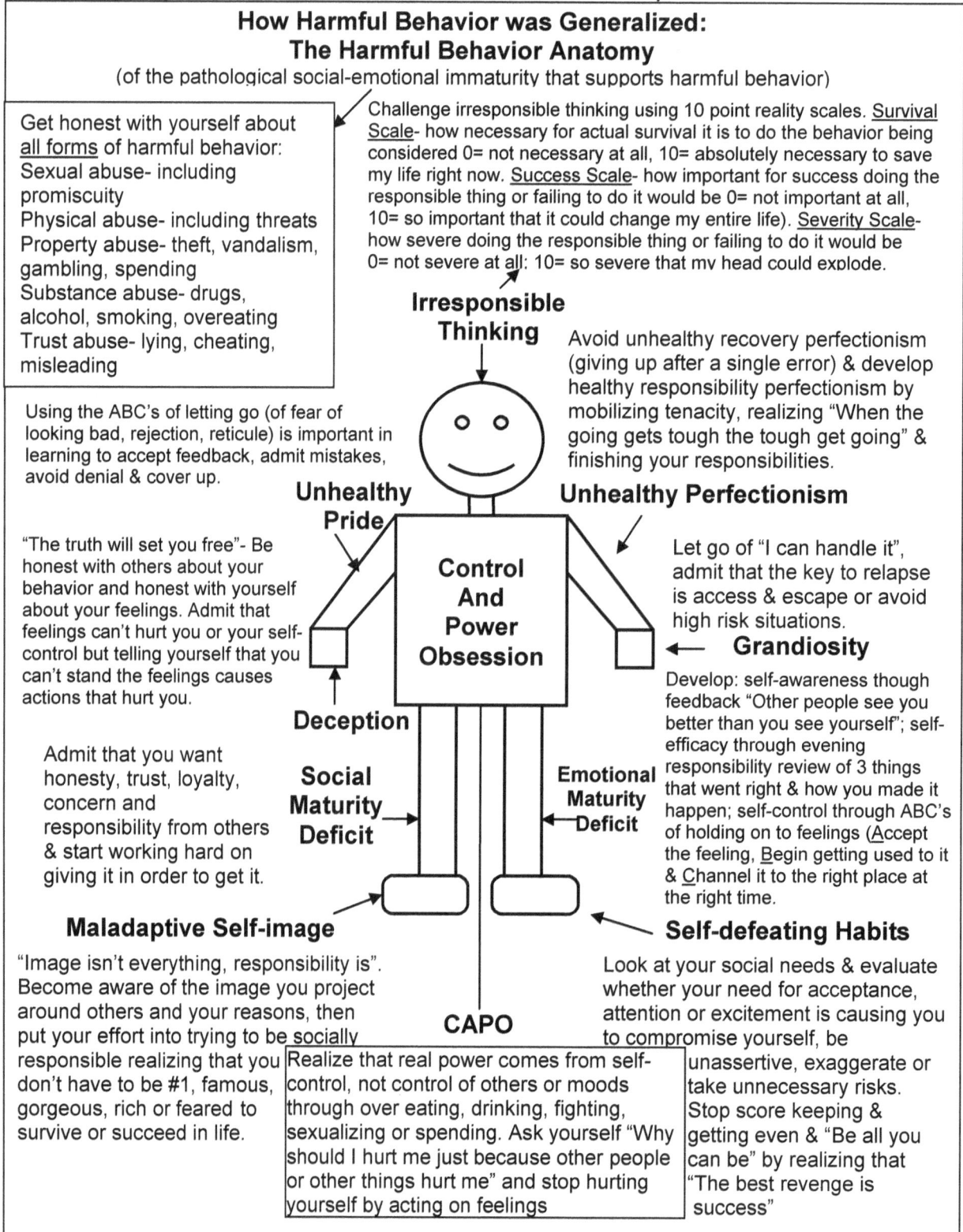

How Harmful Behavior was Generalized:
The Harmful Behavior Anatomy
(of the pathological social-emotional immaturity that supports harmful behavior)

Get honest with yourself about all forms of harmful behavior:
Sexual abuse- including promiscuity
Physical abuse- including threats
Property abuse- theft, vandalism, gambling, spending
Substance abuse- drugs, alcohol, smoking, overeating
Trust abuse- lying, cheating, misleading

Challenge irresponsible thinking using 10 point reality scales. Survival Scale- how necessary for actual survival it is to do the behavior being considered 0= not necessary at all, 10= absolutely necessary to save my life right now. Success Scale- how important for success doing the responsible thing or failing to do it would be 0= not important at all, 10= so important that it could change my entire life). Severity Scale- how severe doing the responsible thing or failing to do it would be 0= not severe at all: 10= so severe that my head could explode.

Irresponsible Thinking

Using the ABC's of letting go (of fear of looking bad, rejection, reticule) is important in learning to accept feedback, admit mistakes, avoid denial & cover up.

Avoid unhealthy recovery perfectionism (giving up after a single error) & develop healthy responsibility perfectionism by mobilizing tenacity, realizing "When the going gets tough the tough get going" & finishing your responsibilities.

Unhealthy Pride

Unhealthy Perfectionism

"The truth will set you free"- Be honest with others about your behavior and honest with yourself about your feelings. Admit that feelings can't hurt you or your self-control but telling yourself that you can't stand the feelings causes actions that hurt you.

Control And Power Obsession

Let go of "I can handle it", admit that the key to relapse is access & escape or avoid high risk situations.

Grandiosity

Deception

Admit that you want honesty, trust, loyalty, concern and responsibility from others & start working hard on giving it in order to get it.

Social Maturity Deficit

Emotional Maturity Deficit

Develop: self-awareness though feedback "Other people see you better than you see yourself"; self-efficacy through evening responsibility review of 3 things that went right & how you made it happen; self-control through ABC's of holding on to feelings (Accept the feeling, Begin getting used to it & Channel it to the right place at the right time.

Maladaptive Self-image

"Image isn't everything, responsibility is". Become aware of the image you project around others and your reasons, then put your effort into trying to be socially responsible realizing that you don't have to be #1, famous, gorgeous, rich or feared to survive or succeed in life.

CAPO

Realize that real power comes from self-control, not control of others or moods through over eating, drinking, fighting, sexualizing or spending. Ask yourself "Why should I hurt me just because other people or other things hurt me" and stop hurting yourself by acting on feelings

Self-defeating Habits

Look at your social needs & evaluate whether your need for acceptance, attention or excitement is causing you to compromise yourself, be unassertive, exaggerate or take unnecessary risks. Stop score keeping & getting even & "Be all you can be" by realizing that "The best revenge is success"

Appendix A.
Information for Mental Health Professionals

Case examples and intervention descriptions in this workbook are provided in "Social Responsibility Therapy for Adolescents & Young Adults: A Multicultural Treatment Manual for Harmful Behavior" (see p. 141). Clinician instructions on using this workbook are provided in "The Clinician's Guide to Social Responsibility Therapy: Practical Applications, Theory and Research Support " (p. 119). Originally developed for client use with therapist input to help those in treatment become more active participants, this workbook provides the high level of structure needed for clients in institutions or residential care where more self-directed workbook structured discovery is necessary. This structured discovery workbook can also provide self-awareness homework assignments for session discussion with outpatient clients in need of structure between sessions and relapse prevention support. The vocabulary bar has been set relatively high for self-help workbooks to encourage cognitive as well as social-emotional growth. This allows therapists to encourage clients whose unhealthy, harmful behavior has interfered with their education to improve their vocabulary by looking up definitions of words that they never learned and sharing them in sessions with therapist prompting. It also give the client practice asking for help on less emotionally charged issues.

Integrating stand alone components- If you look at Figure 1, you will see that there are three sections in The Problem Development Triad: the first has five structured discovery learning experiences on understanding of how harmful behavior was acquired; the second section also has five learning experiences on how harmful behavior was maintained and; the third section has 10 learning experiences on factors that allow harmful behavior to generalize or be substituted for other problem behavior making a total of 20 structured discovery units to cover. These three sections are covered in three "stand alone" workbooks that can be integrated into existing treatments individually. If you are seeking to reinforce the portion of your treatment that develops insight into how clients acquired their condition over time, you can implement workbook one. If you wish to reinforce the relapse prevention portion of your treatment by developing client understanding of how they maintained their problem behavior when others stopped, you can implement workbook two. You can implement workbook three if your client exhibits multiple forms of harmful behavior (i.e., co-occurring disorders) or if you wish to address concerns about their harmful behavior generalizing to other problem areas (e.g., behavior migration to another problem during treatment). However, a solid harmful behavior recovery understanding and emotional restitution through Problem Development Triad presentation on how their harmful behavior was acquired, maintained and generalized will require Structured Discovery learning during the completion of all three workbooks.

Group therapy- If you are running a treatment group or program where individuals start treatment at different times, the three workbooks can be completed in any order but require an introduction session before each which has an overview of the Problem Development Triad. As in individual/family therapy a summary of what has been learned is needed at the end of each section along with one presentation session per person in treatment. In group therapy sessions that are time limited (e.g., 1 ½ hours per session for 6- 8 members), it may not be possible to cover all issues for all clients so prioritize by making sure you cover the top three first. This can be done easily by asking each group member to list several section (i.e., link in workbook 1, phase in workbook 2 or component in workbook 3) descriptors that they rated highest and most important to their recovery. Hold one session for each section where the topic of discussion is the characteristics that were rated highest in that section. Reinforce the healthy relationship success skills (p. 10- 11) and teach the healthy behavior success skills (p.12- 16) as indicated. Create "instant identification" by pulling together similarities with a show of hands, e.g., "Who else rated this characteristic as a 2 or above?" discuss those common characteristics. Then move on to the next person asking for three that haven't been discussed. Usually after several people have talked in a group of 6- 8, the top symptom of that component has been covered for each group member and the group can be moved to processing how that problem affected their life and to generating one positive coping skill to use for each problem characteristic discussed with the homework assignment of using those coping skills on their Situation Response Analysis Logs (Appendix D, p. 107). Note: A simplified version may have to be implemented by the therapist for low functioning groups and examples are available from www.srtonline.org.

Social Responsibility Therapy Group Process Skills- Since unhealthy, harmful behavior is multicultural, the demographic makeup of Social Responsibility Therapy groups is diverse. Given this situation a set of SRT multicultural group unity development skills was designed for motivational enhancement of client participation in the diverse group setting. A simple "PRAISE" acronym helps SRT therapists remember the social learning procedures used to facilitate groups by... **P**ulling people into the group process-"Can I borrow that from you? That's a really good point we need to discuss" (Making them a part/Integration), (p. 38.). **R**esponsible reinforcement- "That [took a lot of courage, was impressive, etc] let's give him a hand for his… [honesty, trust, loyalty, concern, responsibility]" (p. 33, 105). **A**cknowledgement of contributions- "What they are teaching us is…" (p. 38). **I**nstant identification- "Please raise your hand if you have also..." followed by head count "one, two, three... people here also..." for awareness development (Validation/Recognition), p. 192. **S**ocial mathematics by finding the least common denominator (p. 192) during successive group introductions and when two or more members disclose similar issues- "These two/three have a couple things in common, what are they?/did you notice?" (Cumulative Identification). **E**nabling responsibility, "It's not pick on John time, please raise your hand if like John, you have ever been accused of/made the mistake of..." (setting the occasion for honesty & accepting responsibility). These skills are pulled from Yokley (2008) on the page numbers listed in parentheses after each skill above and are described further in "The Clinician's Guide to Social Responsibility Therapy: Practical Applications, Theory and Research Support" (see p. 119). These skills need to be modeled for clients by therapists during all discussions of SRT workbook issues and social-emotional maturity issues to develop multicultural group unity and therapeutic participation. All occasions of clients using these skills in group should be verbally reinforced by therapists.

Individual/family therapy- If you are doing individual/family therapy where everyone will go through all three sections consecutively, a single introduction session can be used with a summary of what has been learned at the end of each section and one presentation session making a total of 25 sessions. Problem Development Triad presentations take between one and two hours per person depending on the extent of the harmful behavior history. This makes a 25 week program in a traditional outpatient weekly session structure or an eight week intensive outpatient program with sessions Monday, Wednesday and Friday.

Abbreviated version- Social Responsibility Therapy can accommodate an abbreviated version for treatment session limitations that are sometimes imposed by program length or funding source session limitations. In all three workbooks, introduce the topic of each section (i.e., workbook 1 link, workbook 2 phase or workbook 3 component) and start with a writing assignment on "What I know about this topic". Then cover the top three key characteristics or concepts to cover and move on to the nest section topic. This allows covering more than one section in each treatment session. If you do Appendix D Candy Bar exercise, discuss the high risk access in all cases.

Repetition- Implement three repetitions of each section to reinforce learning. For example: 1) have client read and complete exercises in a section marking areas that need clarification; 2) review section with client, translating material, clarifying areas as needed and asking key concept questions; 3) have client teach the concepts learned and share personal information/discoveries with appropriate others. This is often done with: 1) a homework assignment; 2) an individual session and; 3) a group/family session.

Adjustment for special needs- Reading level can be ahead of math simply because reading is used more in the everyday life of many people. Thus is not uncommon to see clients do well in rating all of the characteristics in a section and transcribing their top three to their worksheet correctly but getting the math wrong and showing low average scores next to severe behavior statements with high statement ratings. If you have individuals like this, handle it the same way that you would doing the abbreviated version for time constraints by focusing your discussion on the top three rated characteristics in each component which does not require calculating each component average rating score. Special needs in secure residential or correctional settings may require therapists to sign off at the end of each section under the "Discussed with" heading in order to get required completion certificates.

Self-evaluations- Treatment programs addressing harmful behavior often have their participants review their self-evaluations at the end of each Problem Development Triad section in a group treatment setting with their peers and staff. Promotion to the next program phase or requests for increases in program privileges are typically linked to successful progress in social-emotional maturity development (i.e., honesty, trust, loyalty, concern, responsibility, self-awareness, self-efficacy and self-control). The same process can be used in family therapy meetings where teen privileges are based on social-emotional maturity progress.

Client reinforcement- Staff who have used this manual most successfully in the past with the highest level of participation, provided client accomplishment awards (e.g., certificates of completion for adults which included tangible reinforcement for youth) after the completion of each section. Explaining why you are here in several Risk Factor Chain presentations helps diffuse mandated treatment resentment.

Basic Awareness Training, Responsibility Training & Tolerance Training- During implementation of Social Responsibility Therapy, basic Awareness, Responsibility and Tolerance Training tools are needed to deal with the emotional baggage related to past historical trauma and self-disappointment from acquiring harmful behavior habits. Basic Awareness Training tools include the need to become aware of the Irresponsible Thinking (listed in Appendix C) that enables harmful behavior as well as responsible alternatives that need to be substituted. In addition, it is important to help clients develop an acute awareness of the basic high risk situations (i.e., people, places and emotions) that can trigger falling back into the *Stress-Relapse Cycle* and relapse. Basic Tolerance Training tools include an emotional regulation procedure to help clients let go of their emotions (p. 12- 13), dissipating them so that they do not contribute to the *Stress Build Up* that leads to a *Slip* and *Fall* back into harmful behavior relapse. Another emotional regulation procedure is needed to help clients hold on to their emotions long enough to accommodate to them and take them to the right place in order to avoid displacing feelings on others. Basic Responsibility Training tools include a relapse prevention procedure to help clients escape high risk situations (p. 12). A second important basic relapse prevention tool is needed to help clients with the ongoing responsible decision making that can set the relapse process in motion (p. 13- 14). Awareness Training on Irresponsible Thinking and High Risk Situations is prerequisite to the effective use of the healthy relationship and behavior success skills covered in this workbook (p. 10- 16). As indicated in the "Summary of Healthy Relationship and Behavior Success Skills" (p. 10), during Awareness Training in this workbook on how harmful behavior was acquired, basic Responsibility and Tolerance Training tools need to be used to address the problems that led to harmful behavior, maintained it and helped it spread to other areas. A summary of the basic interventions that need to be integrated into The Problem Development Triad is provided in Exhibits 1- 3 (p. 84- 86).

Appendix B.
Self-Awareness Problems & Relapse: Foresight Deficit Decisions
(also referred to as Apparently Irrelevant Decisions or Seemingly Unimportant Decisions)
 "The road to hell is paved with good intentions" -- John Ray circa 1670

Nowhere is the importance of developing self-awareness and using foresight as clear as in the case of Foresight Deficit Decisions. Foresight Deficit Decisions are decisions made without enough foresight or thinking ahead and awareness of high risk situations. These decisions pave the road to harmful behavior relapse often beginning with good intentions. Relapse from Foresight Deficit Decisions often occurs from Problem priorities or Triage Trouble. Triage is French for "to sort" and refers to emergency room sorting of battle and disaster victims in a system of priorities designed to maximize the number of survivors. Problem priorities involves not keeping the focus on the most important problem first. In terms of harmful behavior relapse prevention, problem priorities involves getting diverted away from "keeping your problem up front". This often relates to good intentions, putting other people or tasks first, forgetting about self and letting priorities slip. This can occur from assuming that good intentions can be substituted for good foresight and planning.

In reality, no matter how good our intentions are, if we don't use positive planning, stick to our recovery priorities (i.e., relapse prevention plan), avoid high risk situations, use Fantasy Fast Forward (p. 93) and the reality scales (p. 13- 14) to think it through and weigh the possible consequences, Murphy's Law will take hold and "whatever can go wrong, will go wrong". Foresight deficit decisions or slips occur in virtually all forms of harmful behavior relapse. The following examples illustrate that the key to controlling harmful behavior is developing enough self-awareness to make relapse prevention decisions and avoid the foresight slips that lead there.

A trust abuse (cheating, overspending) example would be the foresight deficit decision by an individual having partner jealousy problems to stop in a flower shop where an ex-girlfriend worked for two dozen roses to smooth things over (slip #1, diversion away from "keeping your problem up front" by good intentions). The thought that seeing his ex-girlfriend might not be a good idea was immediately replaced by the self-statement, "this would be a good test of our relationship" (slip #2, testing self-control). In the shop, the ex-girlfriend commented about the expensive purchase stating "You must really care" which led to the honest answer that the flowers were to try and patch things up (slip #3, diplomacy lapse). This started a discussion of things that had gone wrong (slip #4, inappropriate self-disclosure) which led to talking about the good times they used to have together which led to being invited over to her place "just for a drink" (slip #5 minimizing). That conversation led to rekindling an old flame which resulted in spending the night and giving the roses to the ex-girlfriend the following morning on the way out the door. Feeling very guilty about cheating, they went online and booked an expensive weekend getaway trip to make it up to their partner which put them back into heavy credit card debt. Thus, the foresight deficit decision to buy roses at a shop where an ex-girlfriend worked in order to smooth over a partner conflict, triggered a chain of events which set the occasion for relapse on cheating and overspending.

90

A substance abuse (food) example would be the foresight deficit decision by an overweight individual in a diet program to turn down the cash alternative and accept a cruise that they won at the office work incentive program. This occurred as a result of telling themselves, "I know there's a lot of food on those cruises but wouldn't it be great to do something nice for the family?" (slip #1, careless exposure to a high risk situation with good intentions). The first night of the cruise, ballroom dancing was scheduled to follow a gourmet dinner. They ordered healthy food and ate reasonable portions but after dinner the dancing announcement included an invitation to a complete dessert buffet in the adjoining room for those who didn't want to dance. Their partner took their hand and led them into the dessert buffet as opposed to the dance floor as was expected (slip #2, failure to communicate needs and plan ahead). Not wanting to be a burden they went along (slip #3, compromising self to be accepted) telling themselves "I'll just tag along but will leave if it gets too much" (slip #4, testing self-control) which it quickly did and they left to sit down at one of the tables stating "you go ahead, I'm resting up for dancing". Their partner returned to the table with two plates, put one on front of them that was filled with all of their dessert favorites and stated "This is for your hard earned work that brought us here". They told themselves, "Why not, I deserve a reward" and joined in as opposed to speaking up for themselves (slip #5, rationalizing harmful behavior through feelings of entitlement). Thus, the foresight deficit decision to accept a cruise trip as opposed to taking the cash alternative triggered a chain of events which set the occasion for a diet relapse.

A substance abuse (cigarettes) example would be the foresight deficit decision by an individual who just quit smoking to go over and say hello to some friends they see sitting in the smoking section of a restaurant (slip #1, careless exposure to a high risk situation with good intentions). Having not seen them for some time, they accepted an invitation to sit down and visit because they felt a little awkward about eating alone anyway (slip #2, failure to implement a concrete face saving exit strategy and justifying actions based on feelings). After dinner their smoking friends all lit up and the smell filled the air reminding them of that great feeling that they used to get from a cigarette after a good meal (slip #3, dwelling on euphoric recall). They were caught off guard and were in a sort of daydream trance thinking about it when asked, "Want one?" with their favorite brand being dangled right under their nose. They remember thinking "Just one won't hurt" (slip #4, minimizing harmful behavior) as they took the lighter that was being passed to them. Thus, the foresight deficit decision to join some friends in the smoking section of a restaurant to catch up on old times triggered a chain of events which set the occasion for a smoking relapse.

A substance abuse (marijuana) example would be the foresight deficit decision by an individual in their first week of residential substance abuse treatment to call their partner without discussing it with staff to reassure them that everything will work out fine (slip #1, diversion away from "keeping your problem up front" by good intentions). This call triggered feeling emotionally threatened when their partner seemed to be getting along fine without them which led to a fear that the relationship would be lost if they stayed in treatment because their partner might find someone else (slip #2, affect impaired perception). Since the focus of their residential substance abuse treatment was on learning to deal with self and contact with outsiders is initially discouraged, this fear was not disclosed to others (slip #3, unhealthy pride) causing Stress Build-

Up which set the occasion for the belief that "I must go over there to make sure everything is OK or something will go wrong" (slip #4, irresponsible thinking and Control and Power Obsession). This led to calling a friend to pick them up and sneaking out during a community AA meeting (slip #5, deception). When they arrived at their partner's place, a party was going on where everyone was getting high but they do not leave (slip #6, failure to exit a high risk situation) because there are only five other people at the party and they assumed that the party was planned for three couples (slip #7, assuming thinking error). This assumption validated up their fear that they would lose their partner if they stayed in treatment at the same time that someone passed them a joint and they felt the need to smoke marijuana to calm themselves down (slip #8, justifying actions based on feelings). Thus, the foresight deficit decision to call their partner for reassurance triggered a chain of events which set the occasion for a marijuana abuse relapse.

A property abuse (gambling, credit card debt) example would be the foresight deficit decision by an individual in gamblers anonymous to take a weekend convenience store job in addition to their regular office job to pay off their considerable gambling debt and deciding to stay after learning they would be running the store by themselves (slip #1, careless exposure to a high risk situation with good intentions). The fact that lottery ticket sales were a large part of the business wasn't considered a problem because their gambling debt occurred at the horse races (slip #2, rationalizing, tunnel vision). The following weekend, a customer won $1,000 on an instant win scratch off ticket and gave him a $20 tip. He told himself that he wasn't gambling because it wasn't his money (slip #3, self-deception), he put the $20 in the register and scratched off $20 worth of instant win tickets. Telling himself that one more wouldn't hurt (slip #5, pushing back the line), he scratched off another one and when it didn't hit, got mad and told himself, "Why pay for something that isn't worth anything?" (slip #4, justifying actions based on feelings). By the end of his shift he had scratched off $50 worth of instant win tickets and didn't have the cash to pay for them. He had to leave the store unattended to go across the street and use the bank machine putting himself further into credit card debt to avoid being charged with stealing on the job. Thus, the foresight deficit decision to stay in a weekend convenience store job that allowed unsupervised access to lottery tickets in order to pay off a gambling debt, triggered a chain of events which set the occasion for a gambling and credit card debt relapse.

A property abuse (theft) example would be the foresight deficit decision by an individual who was just fined for shoplifting to borrow a nice leather coat for a social occasion from a friend at the last minute (slip #1, not keeping their problem "up front"). Finding the friend absent triggered frustration and borrowing the coat without asking or leaving a note because of being late (slip #2, justifying actions based on feelings). Not waiting to find the person or taking the time to write a note (slip #3, feeding the Problem of Immediate Gratification) set the occasion for telling self, "I might as well keep the coat because I already have it and nobody knows" (slip #4, rationalizing). Thus, the foresight deficit decision to borrow a coat for a social occasion from an absent friend triggered a series of events which set the occasion for a stealing relapse.

A physical abuse (domestic violence) example would be the foresight deficit decision by an individual who was warned by their probation officer to stay away from their ex-partner to drop in and apologize for the way they acted (slip #1, "my way" attitude). Upon arriving at the house they noticed there was a strange car in the driveway which triggered immediate suspicion and jealousy (slip #2, affect impaired perception). Telling themselves, "I have to know", they barged in the house without knocking (slip #3, Control and Power Obsession) only to find their partner hugging someone else. Without thinking, they yelled out "Who are you?" only to hear the same thing back which instantly confirmed their worst fears (slip #4, assuming) and triggered an attack on what later was found to be a cousin in town for a family funeral. Thus, the foresight deficit decision to drop in and apologize to ex-partner for their behavior triggered a series of events which set the occasion for a domestic violence relapse.

A sexual abuse (adult and adolescent) example would be the foresight deficit decision for an adult in sex offender treatment to put off their regular lunch time trip to the dry cleaners at the mall on Friday (when the number of potential victims to stare at is minimal) to take a friend having problems out to lunch (adult slip #1, problem priorities) or for an adolescent in sex offender treatment to accept a babysitting job because they were pressured to do it (adolescent slip #1, problem priorities). The adult became overwhelmed with a sexual urge from being exposed to several attractive potential victims as they walked through the mall on Saturday with their dry cleaning and the adolescent became overwhelmed with a sexual urge after they walked through the door to greet the children on their babysitting job saw their potential victims and heard the parents tell the children, "Now you do everything your babysitter tells you" (slip #2, failure to plan ahead). In both cases, they maintained visual contact which triggered a flood of mental "snap shots" (slip #3, failure to exit a high risk situation) telling themselves they were "just" staring to get a mental picture for masturbation later in private and had no intent to touch the person (slip #4, pushing back the line). The result was that the adult found themselves automatically following someone out into the parking lot and the adolescent found themselves deciding to give one of the children a bath. Thus, the foresight deficit decision of the adult to postpone a regular dry cleaning trip in order to help a friend out or the adolescent to accepting a babysitting job to help an adult out started a chain of events which set the occasion for a sexual abuse relapse.

Fantasy Fast Forward

Foresight Deficit Decisions can be avoided by using "Fantasy Fast Forward". Fantasy Fast Forward involves viewing the situation you are considering (often a favor or something that involves good intentions) like a movie with you as the main character. Run it through your mind and fast forward to think ahead. Play the movie through to the end in your mind, stop at each decision step and ask yourself "In the worst case what could happen if I take this step?" Use a Reality Check (p. 13) to consider the consequences and determine whether to go ahead or tell yourself "I'm not falling into that" and change your course.

Appendix C.
Types of Irresponsible Thinking & Responsible Alternatives

Irresponsible thinking sets the occasion for irresponsible behavior that is unhealthy or harmful to self or others and prevents you from getting what you want in life. Responsible alternatives requires identifying and correcting irresponsible thinking. This basically involves learning to talk to yourself like someone who really cares about you. If you were standing next to your most responsible and best friend in the whole world in a high risk situation for relapse, they would encourage you to do the right thing and steer you towards a responsible behavior. Talking to yourself like your own best friend involves asking yourself "what would someone who really cares about me, tell me to do?" Although most of us know our best friends really well, since we can't actually read minds, one easy way to talk to yourself like your own best friend, steer yourself away from irresponsible, harmful, negative behavior and towards a responsible, helpful, positive alternative is to "go to the opposite extreme" and do the responsible, helpful opposite.

1. Deception- Examples include… Outright Lying (not being truthful to others) or covering up and avoiding admitting responsibility along with Denial (not being truthful to self), e.g., "It's not my fault", "It just happened", Diversion (changing the subject, disclosing a minor problem to avoid discussion of a major one, shifting the focus to unnecessary facts, details, other problems or people, "They started it") & Division (misleading & splitting people against each other, often into camps that defend or challenge your innocence, "I really didn't do anything wrong"). Vagueness, Dishonesty by omission & Legitimizing (leaving out critical information or misleading with partial information to avoid consequences), A lack of understanding about the difference between dishonesty by omission (withholding information for selfish reasons) and diplomacy (withholding information for unselfish reasons) can also cause problems. Appeasing (telling people what they want to hear), Assenting (agreeing without meaning it and having no intention to comply). Bending the truth to meet needs for attention (e.g., exaggerating a story for entertainment, bragging), acceptance (e.g., gossiping to fit in, giving insincere complements) or excitement (e.g., saying whatever it takes to get someone to have sex) can result in harm to both self and others. Deception which involves basic honesty deficits (not enough) is only one side of the coin. Honesty problems can also involve excesses (too much). Angry over-disclosure of truthful and painful details (brutal honesty) that hurt another's feelings is the most common example. In addition, inappropriate self-disclosure (excessive honesty) for the situation due to social anxiety (nervous talking) can end up hurting you. Disclosing confidential information when asked about someone else (excessive honesty) can result in harm to others. Whether the honesty issues involve a deficit or excess, the results are still harmful to self or others.

Helpful opposite- Get Honest. "Honesty is the best policy" (Miguel de Cervantes, 1547-1616). Admit that the reason honesty is valued so much is the tremendous price attached. Help yourself get honest by realizing that getting honest and taking responsibility is having the courage to face consequences and take pride in your courage to get honest. Use the ABC's of letting feelings go to "Calm down" (see p. 12) so that you don't justify your actions (lying) based on your feelings (fear of consequences). Before you use deception, "Think it through" using the reality scales (p. 13) to weigh out the severity of the consequences to yourself and others. Get honest about your mistakes and the mistakes of others right away to help yourself and others avoid getting in worse trouble later. Tell yourself the truth about the feelings that others could have about your actions and how you feel about the actions of others.

Then avoid stress buildup that can trigger relapse by talking out mistakes and feelings with a therapist or someone who is responsible.

2. Double standards- Examples include… No concept of social exchange where there is an expectation that good deeds are returned & favors are repaid. Everything is one sided. "Do as I say, not as I do". Honesty double standards, not being completely honest and refusing to admit responsibility while telling yourself others "should" level with you. Being more honest with others about their behavior than you are with yourself about yours or being more honest with yourself than you are with others. Trust double standards- Believes they are trustworthy but distrusts others. Has "Trust Entitlement", feels entitled to be trusted (and receive associated privileges based on "innocent until proven guilty" rationalization) despite lack of responsibility but unwilling to trust others. Doesn't understand that trust must be earned by consistent honesty and responsible action. Loyalty double standards involve shifting loyalties and cheating but expecting or demanding loyalty from others. Concern double standards, taking more than you give, being selfish while complaining about, expecting or demanding concern from others. Being a selfish friend or life partner by looking for support and affection without looking for the opportunity to provide it. Responsibility double standards, being irresponsible while complaining about, expecting or demanding responsibility from others. Respect double standards- being disrespectful while complaining about, expecting or demanding respect from others. This can relate to a 2:1 input/output multiplication/division problem occurs when feedback from others is viewed as twice as critical as it was & statements to others are viewed as half as critical as they were. This is because of hypersensitivity to what comes in (magnifying it, multiplying by 2), expecting it to be criticism, aversive or disrespectful in nature (e.g., Viewing "I don't think I agree" as "You turned on me" or "You stupid ass…") & being insensitive to what is let out in terms of criticism, aversive or disrespectful comments (minimizing it, dividing by 2) often due to a role reversal deficit and not putting self in other peoples shoes, e.g., Stating "You back stabbing ass…." or "You dumb ass…" as opposed to "This is important to me so I'd like to know why you don't agree". Viewing disagreement as disrespect and using fear or manipulation to get agreement. In summary, either showing more respect and consideration for yourself than you do for others or showing more respect and consideration for others than you do for yourself. Behavioral double standards- Mistakes you make are considered accidents but mistakes others make are assumed to be on purpose. In parenting, "Do what I say, not what I do".

Helpful opposite- Treat others the way you want to be treated. Use your healthy relationship success skills (p. 11) and practice social exchange by returning favors, compliments, respect and social responsibility (i.e., honesty, trust, loyalty, concern and responsibility). Hold yourself to the same standards that you expect from others. Realize that others are likely to give you the same thing that you give to them. This means being aware of the fact that humans can easily fall into double standards and avoiding double standards in honesty, trust, loyalty, concern and responsibility. Letting go of double standards means having the courage to correct yourself after a mistake in honesty, trust, loyalty, concern or responsibility. Use the reality scales to help you "Think it through" (p. 13) and realize that you can handle correcting yourself after a mistake.

While all double standards are important to work on, trust double standards is particularly important since many people feel that they can be trusted but do not trust others. While trust double standards may relate to years of exposure to television news covering the scandals if those who are not trustworthy, it is still an important issue because "Every kind of peaceful cooperation among men is primarily based on mutual trust and only secondarily on institutions such as courts of justice and police" (Albert Einstein, 1879-1955). Help yourself build trust in others by realizing that there is something in it for you. Realize that you get more privileges as a youth and promotions as an adult "after" you develop trust by being responsible. The key word here is "after". Trust is not a legal right, where you are innocent until proven guilty so don't tell yourself "they should trust me until I prove myself untrustworthy". Since you don't trust others that you don't know well, you can't expect others to trust you without first getting to know you. Just like others have to earn your trust, you have to earn theirs. The point that others are likely to give you the same thing you give them is easy to see with honesty. If you are dishonest with others, they are likely to be dishonest with you. This point can be a little confusing in terms of *building trust* unless you realize that responsibility is involved. If you are responsible with others (i.e., do what you say, when you say for the reason you say), they are likely to trust you and if others are responsible with you, you are likely to trust them. The same thing applies with *learning to trust* which can also be confusing unless you realize that honesty is involved. If you pick honest people to trust and open up with your honest feelings to them, they are likely to view you as an honest person and open up with their honest feelings to you. Picking an honest person to trust is the key here.

3. Irresponsible Loyalty- Examples include… Forming negative ties, developing relationships with irresponsible others. Being loyal to people you can't count on and who get you in trouble by telling you what you want to hear not what you need to hear or asking you to do something wrong. Unhealthy dependency on people who can't be depended on, continuing to give more than you get, overly loyal, remaining in relationships with others who are not dependable or shifting loyalty, problems with attachment and getting close and staying close. Holding Negative contracts, i.e., "I'll cover up your wrong doing if you cover up mine". Defending negative peers. Also includes misplaced loyalty, putting negative peers over positive family or negative family over positive peers. Whether the loyalty issues involve a responsible loyalty deficit (not enough loyalty to the right people or what you know is right) or irresponsible loyalty excess (too much loyalty to the wrong people what you know is wrong), the results are still harmful to self or others.

   Helpful opposite- Practice Responsible Loyalty. Be loyal to those who have earned it through their track record of honesty, trustworthiness, concern and responsibility. In relationships, "Think it though" using the reality scales (see p. 13) to help you stand up for what you know is right and who you know is right by: 1) not going along with what is wrong just to get along; 2) not compromising yourself and what you know is right to be accepted by others; 3) not covering up for others wrongdoing (the longer they keep doing wrong, the worse their consequences will be); 4) not picking looks over loyalty in relationships and; 5) not picking negative people over positive ones as friends, "Consider loyalty and faithfulness to be fundamental." (Confucius, c. 551-c. 479 BC).

4. Don't Care Attitude- Examples include… Not caring and not sharing. Includes lack of concern for self by not thinking about consequences before taking action or telling yourself, "I'm only hurting myself". Selfishness- Not thinking about anyone else but yourself. Telling yourself, "Nobody else matters" or "It's every man for himself". Extreme role reversal deficit. Not putting yourself in others shoes or considering the impact of behavior on others. Lacking empathy. Putting others down to build self up. Not sharing with others. Not being socially responsible by being your brother's keeper and sharing your level of awareness i.e., "I shouldn't have to point out problems that others need to change. If I hold myself accountable, that should be enough" A "don't care attitude" about others by those who only care about themselves is only one side of the coin. Concern problems can also involve excesses with some who have more concern for others than themselves, compromising themselves for others, centering their life around others and thus not really caring enough for self (i.e., "don't care attitude" about self). Whether the concern issues involve a deficit or excess, the results are still harmful to self or others.

Helpful opposite- Show the courage to care, share and try- Take care of yourself and others. Realize that "No act of kindness, no matter how small, is ever wasted" (Aesop, ancient Greek moralist). Let yourself care about what you and do and what is healthy. Help yourself by keeping problems "up front" as a daily priority so that they don't get out of control again. Help others by treating them the way they want to be treated. Push past fears of loss and rejection to let yourself care about others and share your feelings with others who have earned your trust by sharing honest feelings with you. Stop using "who cares" as a face saving excuse not to put effort or energy into getting what you really want. Tell yourself "nothing to it but to do it", push past the fear of failure and try. Add concern to your decision making. Ask yourself, "How will this help/hurt myself or others?" Admit that "If you're not working on the solution, you're part of the problem" and block helplessness by taking responsibility instead of blaming others (i.e., "when you blame other people for your behavior, you give them control over your life"). Use the SET steps to "Solve the Problem" (see p. 14) as opposed to a "don't care attitude" to avoid dealing with the problem.

5. Responsibility Issues- Examples include… No achievement motivation. "I don't need to", "It's not my responsibility", "It's their problem/issue", "I don't want to", puts off doing responsibilities, "I won't because it's not that important", does what they want not what they should. Says they forgot when they ignored it. Not doing their part. Failure to pull own weight. Not "Earning the right to complain" by inconveniencing yourself and finishing a task that was assigned by mistake. Poor work ethic, lazy, "dead beat", borrows and doesn't pay. Feels entitled to top rank pay without starting at the bottom. Includes entitlement dependency attitude, "I don't need to go to school/work" implying that "The world owes me a living". Lack of responsibility motivation involves lack of effort, not finishing what started or finishing but doing half way job. No concept of track record (i.e., telling yourself that you have changed after a few days or weeks when a track record is measured in months and years) is a recovery problem that prevents long term lifestyle change. Puts fun before work is an example of responsibility problem priorities. Also failure to schedule time for responsibilities, and no life achievement goals or motivation to succeed at anything that involves hard work and avoiding responsibilities that are boring or not interesting. Includes "my way" excuses for responsibility refusal, e.g., "I don't have to make it the hard way, I can always… deal drugs, pimp/live off of women, hook/live off of men, go on welfare, depend on my family/friends, gamble or win the lottery". Lack of social responsibility and work effort can be found in the criminal subcultures of societies around the world where realizing that criminal subculture does not represent minority culture determines the unity of these societies. Refusing to accept personal responsibility involving unwillingness to look at ones part in a problem typically involves blaming problems on others or circumstances. Responsibility issues which involve basic responsibility deficits is only one side of the coin with responsibility problems which can also involve excesses by some who take on too much responsibility, do too much for others and blame themselves unnecessarily. Whether the responsibility issues involve a deficit or excess, the results are still harmful to self or others.

Helpful opposite- Accept your responsibilities. "None of us can hope to get anywhere without character, moral courage and the spiritual strength to accept responsibility" (Thomas Watson,

1874-1956). Getting what we want in life requires learning Healthy Behavior Success Skills to **A**void trouble; **C**alm down; **T**hink it through and; **S**olve the problem (see p. 14). These skills help us uphold our responsibility to maintain self-control, make things right after mistakes (emotional restitution), pull our own weight and learn to accept feedback. Accepting responsibility involves understanding that real men and women have learned to do what they should, when they should for the reason they should. Don't wait for someone to do it for you, try doing it yourself. Take initiative, look for things that need to get done and do them, start your responsibilities without being told and accept reminders. Realize that the only responsible answer when being reminded is, "thank you, I'll take care of that". If you want a break, earn it by finishing what you started or getting to a reasonable quitting point first. Don't get overwhelmed by too much to accomplish. Know that you will get things done if you learn to set and achieve small but realistic goals one at a time. Get honest about being responsible. Admit to yourself that being responsible builds trust which gets you what you want in terms of favors, privileges or promotions. Accept that our number one responsibility is self-control and use "the 3 G's" (i.e., the three-step social responsibility plan, p. 12) to get out of high risk situations and maintain self-control.

6. Blind Ambition- Examples include… Selfishly getting what you want at any cost and not being able to see (being blind to) or consider anything else, including impact on others. "I want what I want when I want it, nothing else matters". In socially irresponsible needs gratification or career achievement, "The ends justify the means" by getting what you want at the expense of others or by putting others at risk for harm. Putting self and career over everything else including family responsibilities, being a selfish "workaholic". Includes flawed definition of achievement and success, using survival as an excuse to exploit others, profit illegally and be a greedy "takeaholic". Putting money over everything. Compromising yourself or your values to get ahead. Being unwilling to accept achievement alternatives that are socially responsible but either require more work or are less rewarding. Blind ambition also includes having "all or nothing thinking" about achievement, ambition or success by adopting an attitude that, "You're either a hero or a zero" or "Second best is the first loser". This thinking focuses you so intensely on ambition that you lose sight of the impact of your behavior (or your absence) on others.

      Helpful opposite- Show Socially Responsible Achievement. Examples include looking at possible consequences to self and others not just what you want no matter what. Realize that "You're #1 but there are other numbers" and while it is important to take care of yourself, you have the social responsibility to avoid harming others. Look for win-win solutions where there is benefit for yourself and others. Admit that since doing the right thing takes more effort, you value it more & feel better about it. Ask yourself who really helped you in your life and take on the social responsibility to help someone else. Use the reality scales (p. 13) to weigh what it takes for your success against the severity of what could happen to others. Let go of your all or nothing thinking about ambition, achievement and success. Include "being a better person" by improving your an honesty, trust, loyalty, concern and social responsibility in your personal success goals.

7. Motivational Blindness- Examples include not being aware of why you do what you do. <u>Lacking awareness</u>- Not being aware of feelings that trigger behavior (e.g., anger, anxiety or depression); thoughts that trigger behavior (e.g., using words like "should" or "must" which trigger reactions) or needs that trigger behavior (e.g., for power, acceptance, attention or excitement). Unable to identify and label types of feelings or types of irresponsible thinking. Found yourself saying "I don't know" when asked why you did what you did. Motivational blindness is often reflected by statements like, "It just happened". <u>Lacking understanding</u> about how you got the problem, what maintained it and how it spread to other problems or parts of your life. <u>Closed minded</u>, only paid attention to what you wanted to hear or people who wouldn't bring up your problems. You never really knew you had problems with awareness, understanding and openness. You have heard others say you were "clueless" or therapists say "They don't even know that they don't even know" about you.

       Helpful opposite- Develop your Awareness and Insight. Adopt the "Mirror Concept" (p. 105) that "Other people may see you better than you see yourself" and use other people's feedback as a mirror to see yourself. Slow down your reactions and let yourself feel. Then label those feelings. Look at what triggered them to determine where you are coming from with the action you are considering to decide if you really want to take that action. Learn about the Risk Factor Chain that led up to your unhealthy, harmful behavior, the Stress-Relapse Cycle that maintained it and the Harmful Behavior Anatomy that generalized it to other forms and life areas.

8. "I can't" belief (Opposite of Grandiosity)- Examples include… Two basic types- A. <u>Defeatist attitude</u> involving low self-efficacy (confidence) and insecurity. Doesn't believe in abilities. Has unrealistic negative self-appraisal, may be competent but lacks confidence. Doesn't think they are as capable as they actually are, "I can't do it" or "I won't succeed" belief. Feels inferior to others, helpless. Has fear of failure. Afraid to try new things or extend self socially to new people. Extreme pessimism. Always expecting the worst of self and others. Obsessing on the negative. When evaluating the feedback of others, discounting positive feedback and focusing on the negative feedback. "I can't" and "I quit" attitude. Making things fit the "I can't" belief by devaluing accomplishments or discounting achievements. B. <u>Resistance to change</u> involving "Hole punching", telling why solutions won't work without trying them or saying they already did when they heard about it but never really gave it a serious try. Says "I can't" when really means "I won't". Gives excuses for not trying.

       Helpful opposite- Build your self-confidence. Get honest about the fact that "I can't" may be true but it is really true if you don't get up the courage to try. Start by looking at why you won't try. For example, some people are afraid to try because they are afraid they will fail so they tell themselves "I can't do it so why even try". Others are afraid to put in 100% because if they do their best and don't make it, they are worried about being thought of as a loser or failure. These are excuses to avoid putting in effort to succeed. Get honest with yourself, lose the excuses and put in the effort. Tell yourself the truth. If you try your hardest and don't make it this just means, you didn't succeed at one thing, not that your whole life is a failure. Stop magnifying (p. 105) and start working on the problems in your life. Realize that "If you are not working on the solution, you are part of the problem" and start using your SET problem solving tools (p. 14) to reach your goals.

9. Grandiosity (Opposite of "I can't" Belief)- Examples include… <u>Extreme optimism</u> and unrealistic positive appraisal of self and abilities Discounting constructive feedback from others. Other people notice my abilities and mess with me because they are jealous "haters". Thinks they are more capable than they are. Feels superior to others, arrogant. Overconfidence in abilities, "I can pull this off", "I won't get caught" or "no one will know". "I don't have to avoid high risk situations, I can handle them". "I don't have to plan ahead to avoid problems because I can talk my way out of anything that happens". Highly unrealistic expectations, impatient and intolerant of "stupidity" and sense of entitlement based on view of self as unique and special, e.g., "If I want it, they will want to give it to me" or "Because I like her, she must like me". Extreme entitlement to special attention, privileges, rule exceptions, as a result of uniqueness (e.g., "This doesn't apply to me") or superiority (e.g., "rules are for fools who need others to tell them what to do"). Highly confident but may lack competence.

Helpful opposite- Be Realistic- about what you want, what you need and what people should do for you. Realize that while everyone wants some recognition, no one needs it to survive and no one is likely to recognize your abilities if you don't demonstrate a consistent track record and bring it to their attention. Telling yourself, "They should" recognize my abilities, what I've done, etc, is assuming that others do not have their own world of worries to address. Grandma had a saying about making others aware of your accomplishments, "You've got to toot your own horn because nobody else will". In life, "First do it, then point to it". Be realistic about what you can and can't do. When it comes to doing things you know you shouldn't, get honest about the fact that "no one will know" is usually not true but "Three can keep a secret if two of them are dead" (Benjamin Franklin) is usually true and don't do it. Use the reality scales (see p. 13) to keep grandiosity in check and keep you in touch with the reality of the possible consequences of your actions to yourself and others. Don't over-estimate your self-control ability. Get honest about the fact that staying in high risk situations is likely to trigger relapse and escape trouble with "the 3 G's" (i.e., your three-step responsibility plan, p. 12). Continue to tell yourself that you can do anything that you put your mind to but accept that just thinking about it will not make it happen.

10. Control Issues- Examples include… "I must be in control" attitude, starting power struggles for fun and to gain control. Plays people against people, rules against rules and concepts against concepts (e.g., being honest vs. being polite to people) to try and get own way. Has attitude of entitlement to do what they want, when they want for the reason they want. Follows Irresponsible Behavior Law, i.e., "What's right is what I want to do and the reason it's right is because I want to do it". Has "Baby My Way" (BMW) fits when they don't get what they want, when they want for the reason they want and reckless BMW driving crashes their relationships. Uses Winning by Intimidation, outbursts to stop others from confronting your behavior, manipulation or any means necessary to get control, continue to do what you want and have things "my way". Self-control motivation deficit and dysfunctional social values, e.g., "It's only wrong if you get caught", "My behavior doesn't bother me so why should I control it?" Physical & verbal bullying, "It's better to be an offender than a victim". "I give ulcers, I don't get them", "I create fear, I don't feel it". "I control other people, they don't control me". Has attitude that power has to do with being in command of (controlling) others not understanding and being in command of (controlling) self & enjoys dominating or manipulating others. Control issues also involve need to control mood or self-medicate by drinking, drugging, eating, spending, sexual indulging or any method that temporarily controls/alleviates unwanted feelings.

Helpful opposite- Work on controlling yourself, not others. Some people who have feelings of helplessness because their lives have been out of control in the past decide to make up for it by controlling others. Others who have been over-controlled (or abused) in the past fall into the "vampire syndrome" and become over-controlling (or abusive) themselves. Making yourself feel more powerful by over-controlling others results in power struggles or mistreating others and avoids dealing with self. Realize that people who focus too much on being in control could be afraid of feeling helpless often from bad past experiences or repeating what was done to them (the "vampire syndrome"). If any of this applies to you, then conflicts could make you very nervous and too caught up in the extremes of either trying to be in control or trying to avoid conflict. In disagreements or conflicts use the ABC's of letting feelings go to calm down (see page 22) and keep from falling into the extremes of "my way or the highway" or "go along to get along (compromising yourself to be accepted). If past bad memories are triggered by conflicts, remind yourself, "That was then and this is now" and use the reality scales (p. 13) to help you think it through and do the right thing in conflict situations. Decide who you want to run your life, yourself (through decisions you make) or others (who push your emotional buttons and watch you react to feelings they trigger). Get out of those trigger situations, "You need to be laughing and leaving, not staying and stewing". Developing self-control involves using your 3-step social responsibility plan (p. 12) and continually challenging your BMW ("baby my way") thinking, "Why must I always get my way (or always have the last word)?" Weigh out what you are going to say on the reality scales (p. 13) to help you realize that getting "my way" or having the last word is not needed for survival or success and letting it go isn't that severe. Use fantasy fast forward (p. 93) to think ahead by playing the tape in your mind through to the end. Ask yourself, "Is this so important that ten years from now, I will remember not getting my way here?" If the answer is no, let it go. Stop using anger to try and win by intimidation, grow up and admit that anger is a secondary emotion, underneath it you are afraid of not being in control.

11. Image Problems- Examples include… Three basic types- A. <u>Unhealthy pride,</u> Values looking good by being right. Involves unhealthy perfectionism, inability to admit fault, secret keeping and covering up. This is often based on fear of looking bad, stupid, not being accepted or blowing image, by disclosing problems. Reluctant to ask for help, "Keeping up appearances is job #1". B. <u>Criminal pride,</u> Values looking tough/cool. Involves glorifying authority problem tough guy image, viewing kindness as weakness, rules for fools, war story bragging about negative, abusive or criminal behavior and getting over on others, "Being tough is job #1". Criminal pride often involves a fear of being put down and compromising self to fit in, "Being accepted is job #1". C. <u>Superficial values,</u> Valuing what's on the outside (appearance, clothes, jewelry, money) over what's on the inside (honesty, trust, loyalty, concern & responsibility) or who you know over what you know, how you look over how you act. "Looking beautiful/wealthy is job #1". Picking friends based on how that will improve your image or popularity not who is a good person. The superficial values problem of picking looks over loyalty in relationships continues to result in relationship disappointment. All three can involve putting image over integrity, i.e., "Looking good is more important than doing good" and stubborn refusal to back down or change mind.

   Helpful opposite- Be yourself. Examples include not trying to be anyone or anything you're not, just being real about your true thoughts and feelings. Your likes are your likes, your opinion is your opinion and your feelings are your feelings. Unless they are unhealthy or harmful, keep them. Attack unhealthy and criminal pride by being yourself and blowing your image with honesty and humor. Use healthy pride by admitting to self that the reason we value honesty so much is the tremendous cost attached to it. Remind yourself that while "Honesty has its price, the good news is you don't have to pay twice". Realize that being yourself uses less energy which decreases stress build up and improves your life. Don't let unhealthy or criminal pride control your behavior, if you were wrong be strong, back down, stop defending your point, let it go and apologize if you can.

12. Need Problems- Examples include… Three basic types- A. <u>Exaggerated need for acceptance,</u> "I must be accepted" can result in doing too much for others, going along with things that are wrong to be accepted or not be left out (i.e., "going along to get along" and compromising self to be accepted), worrying about how you will be viewed if you do the right thing, tell the truth or if you try something and fail. B. <u>Exaggerated need for excitement,</u> "I love have excitement/must be entertained" or "I can't stand boredom" can result in doing risky, unhealthy or harmful behaviors to break boredom or for excitement/fun, putting what is fun before responsibilities, doing something wrong because it is exciting, instigating to spark a conflict or creating chaos with "Drama Queen" exaggerating and emotional amplification. Sparking conflict excitement- the argument is more important than the issue. C. Exaggerated need for attention, "I must get attention" can result in doing something risky, unhealthy or harmful for attention, "any attention is better than none" and drawing attention to self which overshadows the needs of others to receive social recognition. Can involve getting emotional for attention or support.

Helpful opposite- Get a grip on your needs. Realize that attention, acceptance and excitement are human needs not necessities. Everyone wants some degree of attention, acceptance and excitement in their life but no one needs it to survive, no one is entitled to it as a birth right, no one should entertain you, automatically accept you or devote attention to you without getting to know you first. Don't compromise yourself to be accepted, act out for attention or endanger yourself for excitement. If you want acceptance, accept someone. If you want attention, do something good that deserves it. If you want excitement, try something positive that is new and you have never tried before.

13. Planning Problems- Examples include… Not planning ahead or thinking ahead. Putting things off until the last minute, "Not to make a decision is to make a decision". Like motivational blindness, planning problems can be reflected by statements like, "It just happened". Being disorganized, not writing things down and forgetting to turn work in, being late or missing appointments. Not thinking ahead about the possible consequences of taking an action or failing to do a responsibility. Planning problems also involve a planning skills deficit (i.e., never learning how to put priorities in order with the most important responsibilities first), problem priorities (i.e., putting fun or interesting tasks before more important responsibilities) and pathological priorities (putting harmful but exciting activities first such as drinking, drugging or gambling over more important responsibilities such as homework or child care).

Helpful opposite- Use Positive planning, "Think ahead, plan ahead, get ahead." Examples include playing the mental checkers tape, "If I make this move, they will make that move", "If I do this, the result could be that". Use the reality scales (p. 13) to weigh out the consequences of not planning ahead to get things done. Getting yourself together, means getting organized. Each evening after dinner, whether you have been in school, at work or at home, ask yourself, "What do I need to get ready for tomorrow" and get ready by making a list. Good planners are good performers. Humans perform most poorly when they are caught off guard and good planners are rarely caught off guard. Put another way, "If you fail to plan, you plan to fail". With respect to learning social responsibility, accept that "Accidents happen, behaviors are planned and consequences are earned". Use your three SET steps (p. 14) to make success plans for important life goals.

14. Boundary Problems- Examples include… Five basic types: A. Relationship boundary problems- Not enough boundaries, too accepting, highly trustworthy so overly trusting (assumes others are also), getting too involved too quick, violating personal space, touchy feely. Boundaries too defended, problems trusting and/or untrustworthy, too distant, too quick to push away, reject. Approach-avoidance in relationships, getting too close, too fast, scaring self then pulling too far away too fast. Ownership jealousy- viewing a person as property that you own. Objectifying- viewing others as objects to use to get what you want (e.g., sexual abuse). B. Personal boundary problems- Not respecting personal privacy. Nosey, snooping through others possessions, letters, diary wallet, purse, etc. Trying to be in on everything, eavesdropping or dipping into private conversations, asks inappropriate personal questions. Discloses inappropriate personal information, "Group Leaking", violates group/family therapy confidentiality boundaries (trust abuse). C. Social boundary problems- Viewing elders or superiors as peers or potential partners. Dressing inappropriately for age or setting. Poser-Acting like a member of a different culture or group. D. Property boundary problems- Property ownership attitude. Theft, borrowing without permission, not returning borrowed property, "What's mine is mine and what's yours is mine" (property abuse), "Give me that!" E. Emotional boundary problems- Doesn't respect other people's feelings by going too far with arguing, teasing, horseplay or personal comments. Whether the boundary and trust issues involve a deficit or excess, the results are still harmful to self or others.

Helpful opposite- Show Respect. Treat people like they deserve to be treated. Respect others personal space, personal property, privacy, opinions and feelings. If you want good relationships, take time to get to know the person before getting too involved. If you want to know something personal about someone, say "Can I ask you a question?" to get them ready. "When in Rome do as the Romans do". This means to respect social boundaries by speaking and acting according to what is appropriate to the setting. For example, if you are at a party and are not Catholic, don't tell jokes about Nuns or Priests. If you want to borrow something from someone and they are not there, don't come back later. Use the reality scales (p. 13) to weigh out how important it is for you to borrow the item in question. If it rates high on the survival or success scales and low on the severity scale (impact on the person you are borrowing from) don't just take it, leave a note and call them as soon as you can. Become aware of your Historical Risk factors in the Risk Factor Chain that led to unhealthy, harmful behavior. Don't transfer your past boundary problems onto present relationships, if you were mistreated, disrespected, devalued or abused put extra effort into respecting others boundaries making sure that others are not treated like servants, property or objects for your personal use.

15. Victim View- Examples include… A preoccupation with injustices, falling into feeling sorry for self and making self miserable in a pity party ruminating on past issues. Dwelling on past thoughts that reinforce feeling like the victim of things that were not fair. For example, thinking about getting comfort from your mother for the overly harsh discipline of an out of control father that she was too ineffective, depressed or addicted to protect you from or leave. In this regard, the victim view involves rumination (dwelling) on the only two things that can't be changed in life, i.e., the past and other people's behavior. This results in helplessness and a tendency to view self as a victim. The victim view includes attempts to elicit sympathy from others and includes problems accepting personal responsibility, blaming others for your situation, consequences and associated behavior, e.g. "I don't deserve this, it wasn't my fault, they got it started". The victim view can involve the attitude that what happened is either never your fault because someone else got you upset or always your fault because you always mess up. The victim view can also involve being the martyr, trying to get attention for sadness and sympathy. "No one understands" or "You don't understand" or are common victim view responses to those who do understand but just don't agree. Feeling rejected and acting that victim view out was expressed by one young man who said, "It's better to be wanted by the police than not wanted by anyone."

Helpful opposite- Hold yourself Accountable. Let go of your preoccupation with injustices and save your anger for the real injustices. Use the reality scales (p. 13) to help you stop dwelling on the past and other people's behavior. The only two things you can't change in life are the past and other people's behavior. Dwelling on these things makes you feel helpless because you can't change them and feeling helpless keeps your victim view going. Take responsibility for mistakes. Substitute the responsibility tape, (e.g., "What can I do to avoid this in the future?") for the victim rumination tape, (e.g., "This crap ain't right"). Take control of your life by taking responsibility for your actions. Remind yourself that "It's up to me" to make it in life and "If you blame others for your behavior, you give them control over your life." Stay focused on what you can change (i.e., the present and your behavior), not what you can't change (i.e., the past and other people's behavior). Let go of victim view thinking that, "You don't understand me" and realize that since humans have the same ability to experience feelings it is more likely that they do understand you but simply disagree with your choice in attitude, feelings or behaviors used in your situation. Admit that in the real world, outside of a dysfunctional family, you get consequences as a result of your poor decisions and problem behavior, not because the authorities are taking their bad mood out on you. Put the responsibility for your decisions and behaviors on yourself. Admit that many times you can avoid a problem by avoiding a problem person or a problem place. Accept that , "the best revenge is success" and use your anger from feeling victimized as fuel to succeed by channeling it into getting ahead and making your goals. "If you believe that feeling bad or worrying long enough will change a past or future event, then you are residing on another planet with a different reality system"-- William James (1842- 1910)

16. Justifying Actions- Includes any form of <u>justifying actions based on feelings</u>. For example, excuses and feelings to justify taking action and avoid taking responsibility for self-control such as "I had to hit him, he really ticked me off!" Justifying harmful actions based on unwanted feelings include hurting others based on anger, hurting self based on depression and avoiding or running from problems based on anxiety. Using feelings to justify taking action and excuse the social responsibility of maintaining self-control of behavior that is harmful to others can be summed up in the statement "They deserved it". Justifying behavior that is harmful to self (e.g., eating, drinking, smoking, drugs, etc) after handling a stressful situation can be triggered by the self-statement, "I deserve it". Justifying actions based on rationalization includes score keeping and getting even and is often the basis for This irresponsible thinking is often based on incorrect assumption that the feeling reflects the way things are which can also occur in justifying actions based on beliefs (or group membership), e.g., global, political, religious or gang murder/war. <u>Payback Thinking</u>, i.e., "They wronged me so I'm entitled to my revenge". This type of justification extends into using relationships for payback, e.g., "You care about them, so I'll hurt you by hurting them" or "You care about me, so I'll hurt you by hurting me". Justifying actions also includes entitlement justification, i.e., "Since they accused me wrongly, I'm entitled to do what they accused me of".

Helpful opposite- Follow facts not feelings. Remind yourself that although all feelings are valid experiences, they may not reflect facts and find out the facts before taking action. If action has already been taken, don't justify actions with excuses, find out the facts and get honest with yourself about what you could have done differently. Realize that payback is a socially irresponsible form of working through anger, hurt or loss. Ask yourself, "In the long run, who really suffers if I do something directly harmful to myself or get caught for doing something harmful to others?" and "Why should I hurt me just because other people or things hurt me?" Use the ABC's of letting feelings go (p. 12) to calm down, then admit that "The best revenge is success" and move on.

17. Extremism (Going to Extremes)- Examples include dichotomous (All-or-nothing) thinking. In achievement (school/work/sports) if your performance isn't perfect you're a failure. This is reflected in statements like, "You're either a hero or a zero", "You're a champ or a chump" or "Second best is the first loser". "Being the best is all that counts so if I can't be the best of the best (e.g., student or athlete), I'll be best of the worst (e.g., druggie or bully)". In relationships, "If they don't accept me, I'm a total reject" or being passive, holding things in until stress builds up and blows up through aggressive words or actions. In negotiation, "My way or the highway" view that you must either win or lose and in discussion, "Either you're with me or you're against me". Extremism can include over involvement (encapsulation) in work or relationships to the extreme where everything else is almost excluded or total lack of involvement and detachment, i.e., "It's all in or it's all over". In personal responsibility, extremism can result in viewing problems as either all their fault (which can trigger anger and blaming others unjustly) or all your fault (which can lead to guilt and blaming self unjustly). In parenting discipline, extremism in can result in being too lenient or too harsh which may relate to shifting back and forth between "Don't care attitude" (p. 96) and "Justifying actions based on feelings" (p. 104). Parenting supervision extremism can result in no supervision at all or no freedom at all.

Helpful opposite- Take a Balanced View. Keep your balance in your life goals, relationships, negotiations and opinions. Be very aware of "all or nothing thinking" and how "Don't care attitude" (p. 96) and "Justifying actions based on feelings" (p. 104) triggers going to extremes. Remind yourself that you don't have to be a hero to get recognition from others, that it is unrealistic to expect everyone to agree with you and don't mistake disagreement on an opinion as rejection of you as a person. Understand that it is impossible to always get your way in life, that everyone deserves to get something out of a relationship and it's important to keep a balance of give and take. Take "all things in moderation", strive for the "happy medium" and look for win-win situations in relationships where there are benefits for all involved.

18. Minimizing (Opposite of Magnifying)- Examples include… Playing down problems (often of self) or consequences (often about not doing the right thing). Minimizing behavior frequency or severity can often be identified by the words "Just" or "Only" (e.g., "I just did it once", "I don't do it that much" or "I only yelled, didn't hit them"). Minimizing problems can occur by excusing actions as something you did when you weren't your usual self, "I was really... upset, angry, drunk, high". Minimizing impact or severity can occur by comparison with more serious problems, "It wasn't as bad as what others have done", for example compared to newspaper articles or TV news on the same topic. Minimizing by normalizing (making it seem normal), examples include, "Lots of people do it" or "Everybody does it so it's no big deal".

Helpful opposite- Call it like it is- Use the "Mirror Concept" to avoid minimizing or blocking out valuable feedback from others. The "Mirror Concept" holds that "other people can see you better than you see yourself" and you need to use their feedback as a mirror to get a better view of yourself to avoid minimizing problems. When a mistake has been called to your attention, don't play it down or blow it off. Look at what you need to do to correct the problem, don't try to correct the person. Use feedback to improve your relapse prevention plan, your promise letter and your self-awareness. Don't block feedback out by pointing out that others have made the same mistake. If they made the same mistake and are calling it to your attention, take it serious. They are <u>not</u> a hypocrite because they have done it themselves, they are an expert witness at seeing it because they have done it themselves. Accept that, "It takes one to know one". Keep the focus on the present and your behavior, not the past and others. Substitute getting defensive with the proper response, "Thank you I'll take care of that" to avoid unnecessary conflict.

19. Magnifying (Opposite of Minimizing)- Examples include… Exaggerating a problem (often of others) or consequences (often about doing the right thing). Blowing things way out of proportion, taking constructive feedback personal. Minor criticism is magnified into "disrespect" that is used to justify retaliation. Overgeneralization to the extreme, often used to justify giving up, acting out or not extending self to others, e.g., "since I broke one rule or made one mistake, I'm failing treatment and might as well quit" (rule violation effect), because one adult mistreated you, all adults will mistreat you. Magnifying "Sorry, I couldn't make it, I had to finish my work" into "I'm not interested in you (or you don't matter)" and then stating "You led me on (or lied to me)" as opposed to "I was looking forward to seeing you (or to a visit) and hope to see you soon". Ruminating on injustices, negative feedback or conflicts to the point where any positive is overshadowed and the negative is magnified into triggering action often by using the word "should" or "must". For example, they "should act the way that I want", they "should not have said that" or "I must drink, drug, smoke, eat, spend, hit, cut or run away to get away from my problems and make myself feel better".

Helpful opposite- Reel it in- Use the "Window Concept" to avoid magnifying feedback from others to the point where you are upset and at risk for acting feelings out. The "Window Concept" involves looking at everything everyone tells you and deciding what to keep. If it's helpful to yourself or others hold it dear to your heart, if it's not, open the window and shovel it out. One way to see the possible benefit of the feedback is to ask yourself, "What if I actually did what the person is saying?" This can make it easier because, "Go to hell!" will not help you but "Shut up while others are talking" will (i.e., we never learn anything while running our mouths). If there is any doubt about whether to keep and apply the feedback you receive, use group consensus (i.e., "If ten people say you're a horse, you're a horse"). Realize that exaggerating problems and stirring up trouble about the behavior of others sends a signal that: you are trying to take the spotlight off of your mistakes; you are a bored drama addict who needs excitement or; a thin skinned insecure person who is hypersensitive to criticism. Ask yourself if you really want to send any of these signals to others. Remind yourself that fighting over disrespect is an admission that you have nothing more valuable to fight for. Use the Reality Scales (p. 13) to weigh out the real seriousness of injustices, negative feedback or conflicts and don't overreact. Use the Reality Scales to put things in perspective and avoid overreaction by weighing out the real seriousness of injustices, negative feedback or conflicts. When a mistake has been called to your attention, don't blow it out of proportion, realize that honest feedback as a way to learn about yourself and grow.

20. Assuming- Examples include… Jumping to conclusions and making assumptions without facts, proof or other evidence to support the assumption. Also involves not verifying your assumption based on initial information by continuing to gather information. Making judgments about others and decisions about actions to take based on unverified assumptions. Not "looking before you leap". Making negative assumptions that because one thing has gone wrong or one error has been made, all is lost can trigger quitting or giving up on self.

Helpful opposite- Verify. Realize that things are not always the way they appear so "when in doubt, check it out." Accept that everybody makes mistakes and don't assume that mistakes were on purpose, i.e., "never mistake incompetence for viciousness". When rumors, opinions or other information presented to you kicks up a desire to take action, don't act. If you are being asked or encouraged to act on unverified information use the proper response, "I need to get back to you about that" and then check it out. If you are made to feel that you must take action right away, be creative and come up with a way to check things out or get other opinions before taking action.

Appendix D.   Summary of Situation Response Analysis

The goal of Situation Response Analysis is to increase your self-efficacy (confidence) by learning to analyze your responses to problem situations and by developing your awareness of the Negative Coping that leads to problem responses. Situation Response Analysis is based on the premise that you need to change your internal coping methods (i.e., irresponsible, immature, maladaptive thinking) in order to change your responses to problem situations and break your stress-relapse cycle through positive coping (i.e., responsible, mature, adaptive thinking).

In summary, irresponsible, immature, maladaptive thinking maintains irresponsible, immature, maladaptive emotional and behavioral reactions which in turn tend to be justified by more irresponsible, immature, maladaptive thinking in a continual self-defeating cycle as follows.

- If you always think what you always thought, you will always feel what you always felt.
- If you always feel what you always felt, you will always do what you've always done.
- If you always do what you've always done, you will always think what you've always thought.

Although we all talk to ourselves, that's how we make decisions and solve problems, much of this is automatic and not noticed unless we pay special attention to it. Thus, at first you will probably not be aware of your self-statements (i.e., thinking) that trigger irresponsible, immature or maladaptive reactions to problem situations. Situation Response Analysis is designed to increase your awareness of your thinking during problem situations beginning with helping you review those situations by recording them on a Situation Response Analysis log at the end of each day when you can analyze what needed to be done differently. Consistently analyzing your thinking, associated feelings and reactions to problem situations will help you develop your ability to do "on the spot" substitution of responsible, mature self-statements during actual problem situations. As you begin to develop positive coping through responsible, mature adaptive thinking, you will notice that you are exhibiting less intense emotional reactions and more responsible, mature reactions to problem situations.

Situation	Response	Analysis	
Date and what actually happened in the situation (the facts). People, places, things, sights, sounds or other experiences that triggered irresponsible thinking, unwanted feelings or unhealthy, harmful behavior urges/cravings.	Your response to the situation. What you said to yourself (thoughts), what you were feeling (emotions) and what you did (behavior- What you said to others and what actions you took).	Your analysis of your response to the situation in two areas: 1) whether it was positive and helpful or; 2) negative and harmful and; 3) what you need to do next time.	
	Thoughts, Feelings, Behavior	**Positive Coping (1)**	**Negative Coping (2)**
		Positive Planning (3) What you need to say to yourself (or do) next time. How you will use Responsible Self-statement Substitution or your ACTS skills next time.	

1. This is what you need to say to yourself or do after the Situation to avoid trouble (responsible, adaptive thinking that prevents unhealthy, harmful behavior. Positive Coping is the socially responsible, mature approach to problem situations that decreases destructive urges, making appropriate social behavior control easier. Using any of your ACTS skills to Avoid trouble, Calm down, Think it through and Solve the problem is positive coping. Remember to use your ACTS in order during a crisis situation because you can't "Calm down" and "Think it through" when overwhelmed by a high risk situation trigger. You have to Avoid trouble by getting out first.

2. This is what you said to yourself after the Situation that led to the irresponsible, immature, maladaptive Response that causes problems for yourself and/or others. Negative Coping through maladaptive thinking includes irresponsible thinking, irrational beliefs, inaccurate attributions and perceptions. Irrational beliefs are unrealistic expectations (e.g., irrational use of "should" or "must"). Inaccurate attribution is responsibility, cause or blame that you attributed or assigned to yourself or others by mistake, for example jumping to conclusions by "assuming" things that can't be proved for certain and acting on them without waiting to find the facts. Inaccurate perceptions are views, opinions and feelings about yourself or others that are not correct, for example viewing the situation as less serious than it really us (i.e., using the words "just" or "only").

3. If you used positive coping- Positive planning involves rewarding yourself for doing the right thing and telling someone about your accomplishment (if in a group program writing an accomplishment award on yourself). If you used negative coping- Positive planning involves responsible self-statement substitution by identifying the irresponsible thinking you used (or actions you took) and substituting the responsible thinking you need to use next time. Write what you need to say to yourself (responsible self-statement substitution) or do next time to avoid falling into problems. Hint: For what you need to say to yourself, review "Responsible Self-statement Substitution 101" (p. 67, 94). For what you need to do, think about which one of your healthy relationship or behavior (ACTS) success skills could have helped (p. 11- 16). Write how you could apply any of these success skills next time.

Be sure to make at least one Situation Response Analysis log entry every day as you will be using what you learned from this log in treatment and all three workbooks.

SRT Appropriate Social Behavior Control Exercise

Developing awareness of high risk situations and irresponsible thinking is the first step towards appropriate social behavior control of urges that can result in harmful behavior. Here are some examples in order of seriousness...

Uncontrolled Urge	Resulting Abusive Behavior
Anxious urge to cover-up mistakes or Grandiosity urge to get over on someone	Trust Abuse (lying, deceiving, misleading, omitting)
Negative mood urge, sensation urge (sight, smell) or peer acceptance urge to get high, overeat, smoke	Substance Abuse (drugs, alcohol, tobacco, food)
Envy urge to take or break	Property Abuse (theft, vandalism)
Aggressive urge to get even or get "my way"	Physical Abuse (punch, kick, slap, threaten)
Sexual excitement urge to have sex	Sexual Abuse (rape, child molesting, peer coercion)

Many people in treatment relapse and commit another abusive behavior as a result of entering high risk situations and using irresponsible thinking as opposed to positive coping in those situations. Here are some examples in order of seriousness…

High Risk Situation	Resulting Urge & Irresponsible Thinking
Getting confronted about doing something wrong or making a mistake	Anxious urge to cover-up mistakes or Grandiosity urge to get over on someone, e.g., "I can't stand the consequences so I have to lie"
Being around peers who ask you to get high with them. Smelling weed, cigarettes or food	Negative mood urge or peer acceptance urge to get high, smoke or eat, e.g., "One last time won't hurt"
Hearing someone brag about what they have and feeling inferior or less than them	Envy urge to take or break, e.g., "They can afford t lose it" or "They deserve it for showing off"
Continuing to stick around and listen to someone who is putting you down	Aggressive urge to get even, e.g., "The need to be taught a lesson" or "I'll show you"
Starring at a person that is sexually attractive or at porno, Listening to sex talk or 900 toll calls.	Sexual excitement urge to have sex, e.g., "It's just sex, everybody does it"

Irresponsible Thinking in High Risk Situations: The Candy Bar Exercise

In real estate, the key to good property value is location, location and location. In harmful behavior treatment, the key to relapse is access, access and access (to high risk people, places or things). Since you must learn to identify and eliminate your irresponsible thinking in high risk situations in order to prevent relapse, this exercise is designed to generate some irresponsible thinking for you to address on your Situation Response Analysis log. Bring in your favorite candy bar and have your therapist sign and date it. You will be using your candy bar to represent your high risk situation as a structured exercise to help you discover the thinking that leads a person to relapse when in a high risk situation. Your self-control goal is to turn your candy bar back in next week unopened with no part eaten. You are to carry your candy bar on you at all times in a place where it will not melt. No excuses will be accepted, if you lost it, it will be assumed that you caved into your urge and ate it. Use your Situation, Response, Analysis Log to help you become aware of the high risk situation triggers (thoughts, feelings) that relate to urges along with the positive and negative coping that you use in when in a high risk situation. Discuss your logs with your therapist or group if you are in treatment. This assignment will be evaluated with equal weight applied to how well you complete your logs and how much of your candy bar you turn in next week. Good luck on learning to become aware of the irresponsible thinking related to urges to eat your favorite candy bar! You may need to use a different object (see note).

Note: If you are in treatment for food abuse, are diabetic, are allergic to candy bar ingredients, have had bariatric surgery which could trigger dumping syndrome or have any condition that could harm you by eating your favorite candy bar, do not begin this exercise without making an informed decision after consulting your therapist about the potential benefits & possible adverse impact of participation. If you are advised to use a different object or an empty candy bar, empty it during a treatment session, discuss the thoughts/feelings triggered by throwing food away and use that information as your first SRA log entry.

Social Responsibility Therapy   **Situation Response Analysis Log**   Name: _____

Situation	Response	Analysis
Date & Description (What actually happened)	**My Thoughts, Feelings and Behavior**	1. Was my response positive/helpful or negative/harmful? 2. What do I need to do in this situation next time?
	Thoughts- Feelings*- Behavior-	**Thoughts:** __ Positive Coping; __ Negative Coping **Feelings:** __ Tolerable; __ Stressful; __ Unbearable **Behavior:** __ Healthy/helpful; __ Unhealthy/harmful **My positive plan for next time is...**
	Thoughts- Feelings*- Behavior-	**Thoughts:** __ Positive Coping; __ Negative Coping **Feelings:** __ Tolerable; __ Stressful; __ Unbearable **Behavior:** __ Healthy/helpful; __ Unhealthy/harmful **My positive plan for next time is...**
	Thoughts- Feelings*- Behavior-	**Thoughts:** __ Positive Coping; __ Negative Coping **Feelings:** __ Tolerable; __ Stressful; __ Unbearable **Behavior:** __ Healthy/helpful; __ Unhealthy/harmful **My positive plan for next time is...**
	Thoughts- Feelings*- Behavior-	**Thoughts:** __ Positive Coping; __ Negative Coping **Feelings:** __ Tolerable; __ Stressful; __ Unbearable **Behavior:** __ Healthy/helpful; __ Unhealthy/harmful **My positive plan for next time is...**

* Rate any cravings/urges to eat, drink, drug, smoke, gamble, fight, get sex (1-10: 1=mild urge, 5=moderate urge, 10=very strong urge)

Appendix E.   Social Responsibility Therapy Self-Evaluation

Do a self-evaluation of your social-emotional maturity progress in each of the areas below.

Name: _____   **Date:** _____

Honesty (check one and explain or give an example): __improved; __problems; __both.

_____

_____

_____

Trust (check one and explain or give an example): __improved; __problems; __both.

_____

_____

Loyalty (check one and explain or give an example): __improved; __problems; __both.

_____

_____

Concern (check one and explain or give an example): __improved; __problems; __both.

_____

_____

Responsibility (check one and explain or give an example): __improved; __problems; __both.

_____

_____

_____

Self-Awareness (check one and explain or give an example): __improved; __problems; __both.

_____

_____

Self-Efficacy/Confidence (check one and explain or give an example): __improved;
__problems; __both. _____

_____

Self-Control (check one and explain or give an example): __improved; __problems; __both.

_____

_____

Appendix F.
Completing Your Harmful Behavior Time Line

Discovering Connections between the Past and your Harmful Behavior
"Creativity is the power to connect the seemingly unconnected"-- William Plomer (1903- 1973)

Complete your Harmful Behavior Time Line form (p. 114) in this order. First record your birth date under "Birth" and your current age under "Now" and write age numbers on the top of the time line as is done in the example of "Pete" (See Exhibit 4, p. 113). Second, record the types of unhealthy, harmful behavior that you did to yourself and others at the bottom of your time line. Review your history of unhealthy, harmful behavior (p. 4- 6). Then review the harmful things you have done to yourself and others (p. 70- 74). This should help you complete the bottom part of your Harmful Behavior Time Line. Be sure to include the primary behavior that was your reason for referral to treatment (p. 6). Don't forget pulling others into harmful behavior (See item 3 on your Harmful Behavior Social Diagram Worksheet, page 42). This should help you complete the bottom part of your Harmful Behavior Time Line.

> **Hint:** If you have done too many harmful behaviors to fit on the bottom part of your time line, then start by listing the top three most serious ones (p. 74). Then list to the ones you did most frequently and over the longest period of time.

Finally, record the types of unhealthy, harmful behavior (and treatment for that behavior) you have experienced at the top of your time line. Review the upsetting things that happened to you in the past (page 21- 26). Then review your Harmful Behavior Social Diagram Worksheet (page 42) and circle the individuals who committed harmful behaviors to you, towards you, around you, pulled you into them or got you started. This should help you complete the top part of your Harmful Behavior Time Line. Review the case example below and then complete your time line.

Harmful Behavior Time Line Case Example- The following case example of Pete, a 16-year-old male with many harmful behaviors is provided to help you: 1) see the basic structure of how to set up your Harmful Behavior Time Line and; 2) see the connections you can make when you look at your time line and think about how your past relates to your harmful behavior. Harmful behaviors disclosed by Pete included: Trust abuse- Chronic lying, covering up, false abuse allegations); Substance abuse- Marijuana, tobacco, referred for treatment of sexually abusive behavior in a residential group home; Property abuse- petty theft, shoplifting; Physical abuse- Multiple anger-based peer assaults and; Sexual Abuse- Nine male and female child victims between the ages of 5 and 11, both relatives and non-relatives (See Exhibit 4, p. 113).

Some basic self-awareness connections made by Pete included awareness of his "Vampire Syndrome" repetition compulsion, involving being sexually as well as physically abused and later repeating that abusive behavior on others. Becoming aware that his physical abuse of others stopped when he stopped being physically abused (moved) allowed Pete to realize that he was using physical abuse to vent his anger. Seeing that this did not happen with his sexual abuse of others which continued after he stopped being sexually abused (right up until he was caught and jailed) allowed him to see the need for treatment and let go of his resistance. The direct connection between becoming trust abusive to cover up his other forms of abuse was also important as was the connection between sexual abuse and property abuse (i.e., putting his hands on people had generalized to putting his hands on their property when he became old enough to go to the store by himself).

Exhibit 4. Harmful Behavior Time Line Case Example- Pete

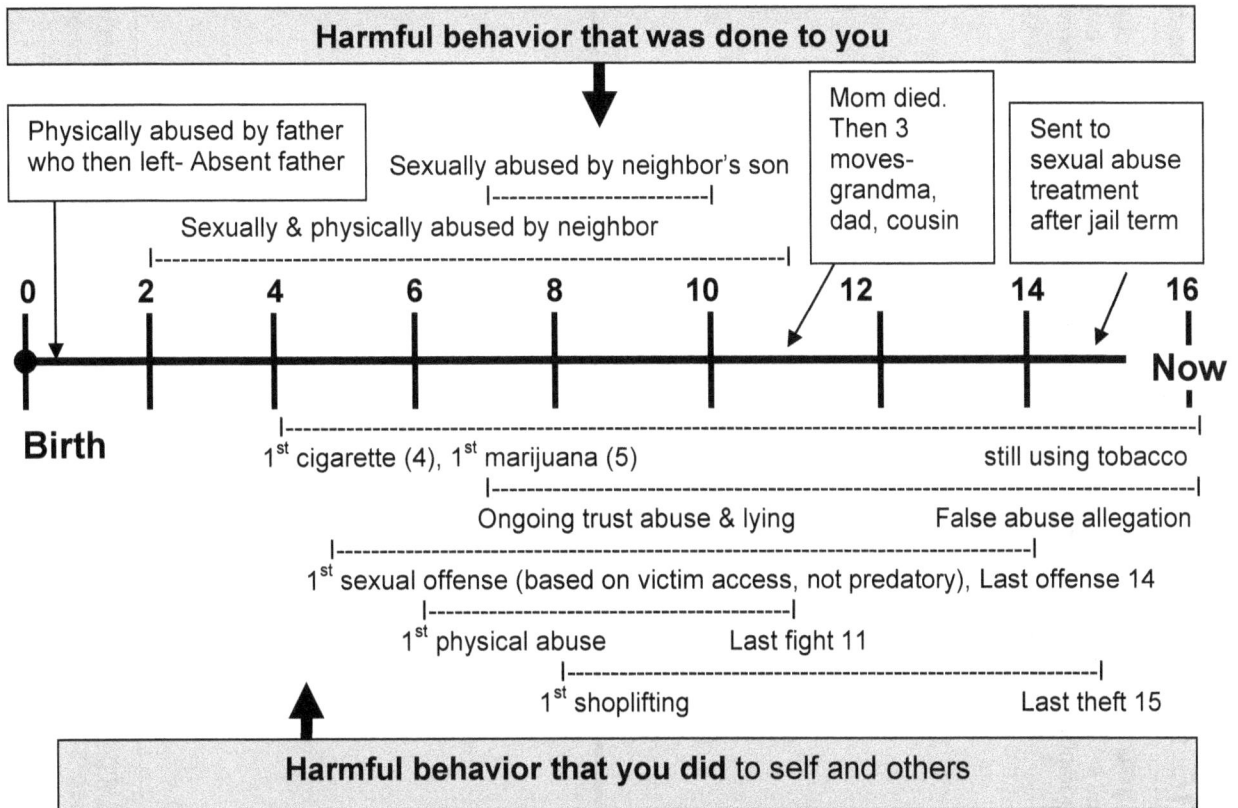

If you need more examples to help you with this assignment, harmful behavior time line examples of individuals referred for treatment of sexual abuse, substance abuse and food abuse (overeating to the point of obesity) are provided in Chapter 2 in pages 128, 129 and 130 of SRT for Adolescents and Young Adults (See Yokley, 2008 in the reference section).

Completing Your Harmful Behavior Time Line

Did you learn harmful behaviors from others? Were you taught harmful behaviors? Did others behavior rub off on you? Document the time line connections that you have discovered in the space provided (p. 115). Look at the behaviors on the bottom of your time line that were harmful to yourself or others and the connections to your hurtful experiences on the top of your time line. Were you using the "Window Concept" (page 77) at that point in your life? Discuss how hurting yourself is revenging the mistakes of others on yourself and when you hurt others, you hurt yourself by risking consequences, holding guilt or both. Learn to use the question, "Why should I hurt me just because other people or other things hurt me?" to avoid relapse.

Harmful Behavior Time Line

Name: _____ **Date:** _____

Appendix F.

Harmful behavior that was done to you (e.g., witness to domestic violence, toxic parents, sexually abused, physically abused, neglected, removed from home, bullied, picked on, threatened, intimidated, robbed, manipulated, incarcerated, constantly put down, had to run the house when too young, alcoholic, addicted or absent parents, loss of loved ones, poverty, multiple caretakers or moves)

Age- 0

Birth
(write ages
above line)

Now

Harmful behavior that you did to self and/or others (e.g., drugs, alcohol, cigarettes, overeating, over spending, self-harm, quitting school/job, negative relationships, sexual abuse, physical abuse, bullying, gambling, theft, vandalism, arson, cheating, running away)

Making Harmful Behavior Time Line Connections

Examine your time line. Look at what you experienced, what was done to you and what you later did. Then write what you have learned about those connections in the space provided below.

_____

_____

_____

_____

_____

_____

_____

_____

_____

_____

_____

_____

_____

_____

Hint: Use the language of responsibility with "I" statements to take ownership of your harmful behavior and don't turn the negative social influence that you were around into blaming others for your behavior. Avoid blaming by identifying who modeled those behaviors by doing them around you, introducing them to you, teaching them to you, or doing them to you while owning responsibility for the choice of whether to adopt or continue behaviors. Put another way, you need to state, "Although I was influenced by my:
  1. (mother, father, brother, friends, etc.) who...
  2. (smoked, overate, drank, drugged, assaulted, molested, etc.)...
  3. around me or got me to try it or did it to me,...
I knew it was harmful and chose to (continue it myself , get others involved or do it to others) despite the fact that it was wrong".

The Harmful Behavior Time Line that you constructed is a picture to help you make connections between your past and your harmful behavior. The saying "Those who cannot remember the past are condemned to repeat it"[5] points out that not only is it important for you to discover the connections between your past and your harmful behavior but to remember what you have learned, "keep it up front" and not forget it if you want to avoid falling back into unhealthy, harmful behavior. The Harmful Behavior Time Line clearly shows your past behavior but can only help you if you use it in treatment to deal with the past issues that are connected to your harmful behavior. An important first step in keeping your issues up front is sharing them with people who will understand and can help. After you have completed your time line, discuss it with your therapist and/or treatment group. Start at the bottom of your time line and work your way up to make sure that you take responsibility for your behavior first before discussing the behavior of others.

Workspace (Label your work)

Social Responsibility Therapy for Adolescents and Young Adults
A Multicultural Treatment Manual for Harmful Behavior
James M. Yokley, Ph.D.

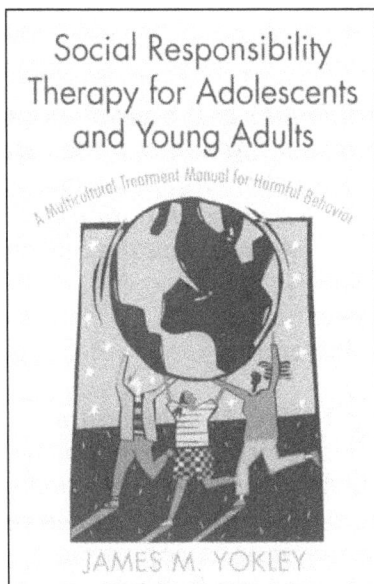

Social Responsibility Therapy for Adolescents and Young Adults: A Multicultural Treatment Manual for Harmful Behavior provides a comprehensive explanation of Social Responsibility Therapy, its advantages, and the intervention evidence-base for multiple forms of harmful behavior. This text discusses in detail the multicultural intervention approach, its rationale, and content. Implementation methods and treatment protocol are explored. The book includes illustrated case studies, tables, figures, and references to additional available readings.

Topics discussed in Social Responsibility Therapy for Adolescents and Young Adults: A Multicultural Treatment Manual for Harmful Behavior include:
- evidence-based procedures used in Structured Discovery learning experiences to target harmful behavior
- helping clients discover how they acquired, maintained, and generalized a broad range of harmful behavior
- addressing target behavior problems, negative social influence problems, and the dose-response problem
- five areas of human functioning that are critical to the wellbeing of self and others which can only be addressed through psychotherapy and forensic parenting
- developing prosocial behavior alternatives which contribute to both relapse prevention and personal development and much more!

Social Responsibility Therapy for Adolescents and Young Adults: A Multicultural Treatment Manual for Harmful Behavior is an essential resource for social workers, counselors, psychologists, and psychiatrists whose caseloads include a multicultural population of young people who exhibit multiple forms of harmful behavior.

Table of Contents
Chapter 1. Social Responsibility Therapy Overview, Intervention Evidence Base and Multicultural Approach. **Chapter 2.** Client Awareness Training: The Problem Development Triad. **Chapter 3.** Social Responsibility Therapy Implementation Methods and Treatment Protocol. **Chapter 4.** Research Support for Social Responsibility Therapy Methods & Procedures. Notes. References.

About the Author
James M. Yokley, Ph.D., is a Clinical Psychologist on the medical staff in the Department of Psychiatry at MetroHealth Medical Center in Cleveland, Ohio, as well as an Assistant Professor at Case Western Reserve University School of Medicine and Department of Psychology. He has expertise in cognitive-behavior therapy with multiple forms of harmful behavior, has authored over 50 research publications, book chapters, and professional presentations, and is a regular conference speaker on this topic.

Paperback: 978-0-7890-3121-1. $49.95 • May 2008, 357pp

Order online through
www.socialsolutionspress.com

Social Responsibility Therapy for Adolescents and Young Adults
A Multicultural Treatment Manual for Harmful Behavior
James M. Yokley, Ph.D.

"A valuable contribution to the field, confronting important issues at the psychological and societal levels. Provides a comprehensive framework for managing some of the most challenging clinical problems. Provides useful guidelines for promoting prosocial values and behaviors in delinquent youth. The treatment strategies balance the notions of therapeutic structure with client discovery. Many interesting and provocative quotations are laced throughout the text. A valuable addition to any library."
—James C. Overholser, PhD, ABPP, professor of psychology,
director of clinical training, Case Western Reserve University

Social Responsibility Therapy for Adolescents and Young Adults: A Multicultural Treatment Manual for Harmful Behavior is a crucial treatment manual for mental health professionals whose caseloads include a multicultural population of adolescents and young adults who exhibit multiple forms of harmful behavior. This unique therapy enhances relapse prevention in harmful behavior treatment by addressing the target behavior problem, negative social influence problem, dose-response problem, and the behavior migration problem. It also acknowledges that harmful behavior is multicultural, and it addresses the key criticisms of multicultural therapy through a theory-driven treatment approach that utilizes methods and procedures from existing evidence-based treatments with known multicultural applications.

This text provides a comprehensive explanation of Social Responsibility Therapy, its advantages, and the intervention evidence-base for multiple forms of harmful behavior. It discusses in detail the multicultural intervention approach, its rationale, and content; describes the implementation methods and treatment protocol; and includes illustrated case studies, tables, figures, and references to additional readings. This book is an essential resource for mental health professionals from all disciplines, including social workers, counselors, psychologists, and psychiatrists who are involved in the treatment of multiple forms of harmful behavior.

James M. Yokley, PhD, is a clinical psychologist in the Department of Psychiatry at MetroHealth Medical Center in Cleveland, Ohio, and is an assistant professor at Case Western University School of Medicine and Department of Psychology.

Routledge
Taylor & Francis Group

www.routledgementalhealth.com

Printed in the U.S.A.
Cover design: Elise Weinger Halprin

ISBN: 978-0-7890-3121-1
90000

9 780789 031211

an **informa** business

The Social Responsibility Therapy: Understanding Harmful Behavior Workbook Series

The Social Responsibility Therapy workbook series on Understanding Harmful Behavior was designed to help individuals with unhealthy, harmful behavior understand how they got that problem, what kept it going and how it spread to other areas through "The Problem Development Triad".

Workbook 1- "How did I get this problem?" focuses on understanding how unhealthy, harmful behavior was acquired through "The Risk Factor Chain". ISBN: 978-0-9832449-0-5.

Workbook 2- "Why do I keep doing this?" focuses on understanding how unhealthy, harmful behavior problems were maintained by "The Stress-Relapse Cycle". ISBN: 978-0-9832449-1-2.

Workbook 3- "How did my problem spread?" focuses on understanding how unhealthy, harmful behavior problems were generalized to other areas using "The Harmful Behavior Anatomy". ISBN: 978-0-9832449-2-9.

The Clinician's Guide to Social Responsibility Therapy: Practical Applications, Theory and Research Support

The Clinician's Guide to Social Responsibility Therapy: Practical Applications, Theory and Research Support (ISBN-978-0-9832449-4-3) supplements the Social Responsibility Therapy Treatment Manual for Adolescents & Young Adults (Yokley, 2008) by providing: Practical clinical applications, case examples and exercises illustrating the treatment model; A positive lifestyle change description integrating theory, research support and practical examples; Clinician support for using the three Social Responsibility Therapy workbooks on understanding and managing unhealthy, harmful behavior described above.

Further description and order information is available at
www.socialsolutionspress.com

For volume or non-profit organization discounts, e-mail order information (Name, zip code and number of workbooks, organization and population served) to...
info@socialsolutionspress.com

Note:

Social Responsibility Therapy is a Social Solutions Healthy Behavior Lifestyle Project

www.srtonline.org   www.socialsolutionspress.com   www.forensicare.org

9780983244905